THE ALMOST TOTALLY COMPLETE

I'M SORRY I
HAVEN'T A CLUE

The contributors would like to extend special thanks to
Emma Darrell, Jill Foster, Susan da Costa, Kate Haldane, Trevor Dolby, Pandora White,
Neal Townsend, Mal Peachey, Paul Merton, Stephen Fry, Jeremy Hardy, Sandi Toksvig,
Tony Hawks, Fred MacAulay, Denise Coffey, Peter Bradshaw, Steve Punt, Robert Fraser Steel,
Janet Staplehurst and David & Shirley Scott.

THE ALMOST TOTALLY COMPLETE

I'M SORRY I HAVEN'T A CLUe

Tim Brooke-Taylor, Barry Cryer, Willie Rushton
Graeme Garden and Humphrey Lyttelton

Funny bits written by Iain Pattinson

Edited and compiled by Jon Naismith

Musical arrangement by Colin Sell (Piano – Grade VI)

ORION

First Published in 1999 by **Orion Books Ltd**.
Orion House
5 Upper St. Martin's lane
London WC2H 9EA

Based on the BBC Radio Programme.
'I'm Sorry I Haven't A Clue' is a trademark of the
British Broadcasting Corporation and used under license.

Jacket photograph: **The Hulton Getty Picture Collection**

Design and layout by **Essential Books**

A CIP catalogue record for this book is available
from the British Library

ISBN 0752811844

Printed and bound in Great Britain by
**Butler & Tanner Ltd.
Frome and London**

Contents

Foreword

Unbeknown to me, there had been rumours circulating of a book to celebrate our favourite wireless programme for several years; however it wasn't until the publishers rang me at home that I first got wind. A good dose of Milk of Magnesia soon put that to rights. Yes, it was true, there was to be an *I'm Sorry I Haven't A Clue* book and would I like to write the foreword?!

My first attempt was not, frankly, a success. Partly because my styping kills aren't what they oozed, Toby, and partly because my rusty shorthand recorded that I had been asked to write the F-word. (On the plus side, the few thousand early editions that were issued with a half-page F-word did sell out within hours. A hearty "well done" to the Christian Bookshop, Ludlow!)

But why should such a broadcasting institution as "Clue" want me anyway? What possessed Lionel and Una to pick my name? Yes, dear reader, you will have guessed that in my excitement, I had confused the long running wireless panel game with the smash hit TV sensation. When the full enormity of the truth dawned, it was exactly like the sun rising in the morning to whisper in my ear what a task I'd taken on, except that it was already teatime and quite overcast, being February, and I didn't actually hear anything.

How could I hope to introduce the book of that show? Well, let's just pause to think what marks it out: regular teams consisting of Britain's greatest after-dinner speaker, a comedy writer second to none and an improvisational actor without peer, all shepherded by the enabling, light touch of a quick-fire chairman. That's what any other show would have had, but not "Clue". So throw off your shackles of convention and enjoy – as the man says every week – the "Antelope to Panel Pins".

Mrs Trellis,
North Wales.

(Editor's note: This foreword won the *I'm Sorry I Haven't a Clue* "Write A Foreword" Competition by dint of being the first of 3,000 entries pulled out of the hat containing the 3,000 submissions of Mrs Trellis.)

Introduction

When the BBC first began broadcasting in the 1920s, there were no radio "comedy" shows as such; programmes weren't intended to make the listener laugh. How different to the late 1990s when there was a whole BBC department devoted to making comedy shows specifically designed not to make the listeners laugh.

Broadcasting House: The morning after the first broadcast of Anderson Country.

The sporadic attempts at comedy made in the early years consisted mainly of jokes inserted into otherwise straight presentations. Sporting events were especially appropriate, although a joke about two sailors scraping barnacles off the Queen Mary's bottom did go down unexpectedly well, and livened up an otherwise rather dull commentary on the state funeral procession of King George V.

The first ever actual joke broadcast was probably this, taken from the transcript of a 1921 commentary on the final test against India at the Oval. The reporters were Arthur Pink and Bernard Lyttle.

Lyttle: With the MCC chasing India's total of 468 declared, our hopes are with team Captain, Donald Gardiner and First Bat, Geoffery Hiscock. And as they take up their positions at the wicket, the crowd roars its approval at the sight of Gardiner giving Hiscock a friendly wave from the gasworks end.

Pink: It was a bold decision of Gardiner to open the batting with Hiscock.

Lyttle: Yes, Arthur, a lesser man might have only used Hiscock later.

Pink: Personally, I'd like to feel Hiscock was going in and staying there all afternoon ...

Lyttle: And as Pootna Shankaranji runs in to bowl the first delivery ... oh my goodness! Hiscock is out! What a terrible sight! Hiscock is out! Held skilfully by the wicket keeper, Hiscock is out for a duck.

Pink: What can Gardiner do now but watch in disbelief as the umpire points Hiscock towards the pavilion?

Lyttle: Well, as we wait for number three to arrive at the crease,

An early experiment in surround sound.

how about a joke to cheer the listeners up? My dog's got no nose.

Pink: But how does he determine aromas?

Lyttle: Not awfully well, I'm afraid!

The Heads of BBC Wireless listen to the hilarious pilot of I'm Sorry I Haven't A Clue *before commissioning the first series.*

This inappropriately timed joke resulted in a furore at Broadcasting House. The two senior commentators knew their joke was a good one, but they were at a loss to understand quite why the entire British Empire had collapsed in tears of mirth. As jokes weren't covered by the BBC Code of Broadcast, an enquiry was held, the report concluding "... with the opening batsman gone, gales of unfortunate laughter resulted at a most solemn stage of a vital test match."

The Director General made a personal presentation of the enquiry's findings to the Board of Governors, his speech partly blaming the commentators but mainly the hapless batsman, whose dismissal had humiliated the nation before the known world.

The DG's summing up: "... as a result, I shall be seeing Hiscock, Lyttle and Pink in my office first thing on Monday morning" was greeted with thunderous applause.

What must be considered the first wireless comedy programme proper was commissioned by Lord Reith in 1926 to help cheer the listening masses during the Depression. The Depression wasn't due to start for another seven years, but Reith was already making plans to introduce one. The BBC formed a "Variety" department to handle the project and its first young producer was sent out to recruit talent from the Music Hall circuit.

Sadly, his early programme proposals found little favour with the conservative Reith. They included:- *The Clitheroe Kid* (the adventures of a young Lancashire goat), *Are You Being Served?* (an everyday story of country folk at an artificial insemination plant), *Dad's Army* (amusing anecdotes from the son of Kaiser Wilhelm II) and *Just A Minute* (Mrs Nicholas Parsons' amusing anecdotes about her honeymoon).

All were rejected, Reith preferring to recruit his own rep of talent that included Jimmy Handley-Page, Tommy Sopwith, Harry Hawker, Freddie Armstrong-Siddely and even some who hadn't been First World War aircraft manufacturers. Their careers with a radio script were limited only by the fact that none of them had ever learnt to read. Hence each of them only ever used a "catchphrase", saying nothing else for entire programmes.

Who can fail to remember those classic shows from the Golden Age of Wireless – and those legendary catchphrases?

The first I'm Sorry I Haven't A Clue *drive-in wireless show at Ruislip.*

Take It From Her "Make mine a large one, Eth"
ITMA (Isn't This Most Amusing) "Can I screw you now, Sir?"
The Navy Lark "Rum WHAT and Coca Cola?"
Round The Horn "I'm Julian, and my friend's handy"
Much B*n*ing In The Marsh "Not in my gas mask you don't" *

Hence, it took the 1945 Education Act to solve the problem of wireless comedy. With the war over, and in celebration of that legislation, the BBC commissioned a new show called

Radio 4's crack team of commissioning editors meet to choose the new schedule.

Education Act Archie, featuring a ventriloquist dummy of such dubious quality that as the audience listened you could see their ears move. This series launched the careers of many future stars, while the unconvincing dummy went into management, ending up as Controller of Radio 4 in the late 1990s.

Apparently, *I'm Sorry I Haven't A Clue* started up sometime in the 1970s. So there we are.

---

* N.B. *If you can fail to remember those classic shows from the Golden Age of Wireless – and those legendary catchphrases, call 0998 098 809 and claim your £5 prize. Calls charged at £37 per minute.*

Famous First Words

In which the teams were invited to suggest the first words of people either still living, or appearing on *Celebrity Squares* ...

- "Nurse, would you mind putting your hand on this"
  President Clinton

- "I'm always going to look like this"
  William Hague

- "Now we are a granddaughter"
  Margaret Thatcher

- "Never again"
  Julian Clary

- "Hello, good evening and talcum"
  Sir David Frost

- "Go ahead punk, cut my cord"
  Clint Eastwood

- "I'll break the waters if you don't mind"
  Charlton Heston

- "As I was saying"
  The Dalai Lama

- "I'm out! Everybody out!"
  Arthur Scargill

- "Those dirty nappies give me a great idea!"
  Mr MacDonald (Hamburger King)

- "Goo goo. Oh, repetition of goo"
  Clement Freud

- "And tell me, have you been doing this job for long?"
  The Queen (to midwife)

- "Goo Goo Gaa Gaa Boo Bop A Loo Ma"
  Little Richard

- "No nurse, that's not the umbilical cord"
  Tom Jones

- "Cut! I'd like to go again, love. Lots more screaming this time"
  Michael Winner

- "You're right Mum, labour leaves you knackered"
  Tony Blair

National Anthems

As the political map of the world continues to change, many nations have felt the need for a new national anthem. In celebration of their new-found independence, the Scots have recently taken to singing "O Flour Of Scotland", that famous romantic celebration of the baking products of Mr McDougall. Other countries have chosen to adapt songs from the popular canon ...

- "Ba-Ba-Ba Ba-Ba-Bados"
- **"Taiwan Yellow Ribbon Round The Old Oak Tree"**
- "You Say Tobago and I Say Tobargo"
- **"Chile Chile Bang Bang" (It's that Pinochet moment)**
- "Dr Finland's Casebook"
- **"If You Knew Zealand Like I Know Zealand"**
- "Turkey Turkey Cheep Cheep"
- **"Never Mind The Balearics"**
- For Australia and New Zealand: "Antipodi-do-da, Antipodi-ay ..."
- **"Crash Bangladesh Wallop What A Picture"**
- "Papua Back Writer"
- **"Pharaohese A Jolly Good Fellow"**
- "I'm Henery The Eighth Siam"
- **"One Man Went To Mow, Went To Mozambique"**
- "It's Jakarta And I'll Cry If I Want To"
- **"Now I'm A Bolivian" (the old Monkees number)**

- "Chim-Chiminee Chim-Chiminee Chim-Chim Peru"
- **For Wales: "Take That Leek Off Your Face"**
- "I Did It Norway"
- **"Sudan You're Rocking The Boat"**
- "The Fog On The Dead Sea's All Mine All Mine by Gazza"
- **"Singing in Bahrain"**
- "Happy Turkey Turkey, Happy Turk"(by Paul Ankara)
- **"Yes, We Have No Botswanas"**

RadioTymes

Just a casual flick through a pile of old magazines can reveal unexpected treasures. Humph recalls coming across an edition of *The Radio Times* dating back several hundred years in just this way. Sadly, he didn't get a chance to read it as the dentist was ready to see him, but the teams were able to speculate on what might have been printed inside.

ANCIENT GREEK RADIO TIMES

- The Hammer House of Horace
- **Theseus Your Life**
- Only Fools and Wooden Horses
- **Menelaus Behaving Badly**
- Oedipus Blind Date, hosted by Scylla and Charybdis
- **Homer and Away**
- Hector's House
- **How Do They Do That? Juno?**
- Tonight's movie – Troy Story (shown at Priam Time)
- **They Think It's All Ovid**
- A Question of Sparta
- **Educating Archimedes**
- The Nine O'Clock Zeus and Medusa Ten
- **Monty Parthenon starring John Cleese, Androcles and Pericles**
- The Goddies with Bill Odysseus
- **Wish You Were Hera**
- This Morning with Castor and Pollux
- **Acropolis Now**
- Sirens Of The Lambs
- **Wooden Horse Jumping from Hickstead followed by cricket and the Minotaur of Zimbabwe**

BIBLICAL RADIO TIMES

- **They Think It's All Jehovah**
- Doubting Thomas – With How Do They Do That?
- **An Audience With Barbara Cartland**
- Genesis Live In Concert
- **Noah's House Party**
- The Fast Show
- **Don't Give Up Your Day Job**
- Three Wise Men Behaving Badly
- **Masterchef – The Feeding Of The Five Thousand**
- Have I Got Jews For You
- **Challenge Annanas**
- Beasts Of The Field Win Prizes
- **Gladiators – The Early Years**
- The Best of Esther
- **Middle Eastenders**
- The Exodus Files
- **Pontius – that was just a pilot**

- It'll Be Alright On The Night So Long As You Slap Blood All Over Your Front Door
- **Frost on Sunday, Locusts on Monday, Boils on Tuesday...**
- Down Yahweh
- **Adam's Family**
- Tom and Jeremiah
- **The Samsons**
- Gomorrah's World
- **Wish You Were Herod**
- They Think It's Passover
- **The Plague Forecast**
- Lord and Masterchef
- **I Love Lucifer**
- Michael Buerk's 666
- **Candid Camel**
- To The Manna Born
- **Luke Whose Talking**
- The Saint

Chat-up Lines

When it comes to romance, the very first words spoken can be so important. The *I'm Sorry I Haven't A Clue* team are frequently approached by women with interesting opening lines. One often addressed to Tim Brooke-Taylor is: "Ah, the good looking one from *The Goodies*. Do you know what became of him?" And Graeme Garden says he's usually propositioned with the gambit: "I didn't recognise you in colour". Barry Cryer's most commonly approached with: "Oi! What are you doing in those bushes?" Every situation develops its own *patois de coeur*. Here are just some of them ...

IN HOSPITAL

- Cough!
- **Do you coma here often?**
- Did anyone tell you you've got a cute angina?
- **My drip or yours?**
- I hear you're looking for a fine specimen.
- **I want you to have my babies ... vaccinated.**
- I must say I admire your guts. Will the doctor let you keep them?
- **Your X-rays don't do you justice.**
- Would you like to see what a private room looks like?
- **Got any glasses? I've found a bottle.**
- D'you know, seeing you in those stirrups, I thought you were Michael Winner.
- **Did the bowels move for you?**
- You've got the most beautiful new eyes.
- **Is your leg up in plaster, or are you just pleased to see me?**

IN THE GARAGE

- I'm going to have to get underneath.
- **I'll just roll you up onto the pavement and then we won't be in anybody's way.**
- What's a nice grille doing in a body like this?
- **Let's play petrol pumps.**
- Why don't we test for emissions?
- **Have you been turning this back? You little clock teaser.**
- You'd expect a bit of rattling on one this age.
- **I'll give you a jump start and that'll get you going in no time.**
- You realise that this thing is just an extension of my car?
- **D'you want to put it in first?**
- Go to bed with me and I'll tell you what's really wrong with your car.

IN CHURCH

- Ha-lo!
- **Would you care to be de-frocked?**
- I can think of something I'd like you to alter, boy.
- **Would you like to be one of the Lay Sisterhood?**
- It's all right, I'm a vicar.
- **If anyone can – the Canon can.**
- I say, now that's a habit I wouldn't mind getting into.
- **Look, I forgive whatever you're about to do with me.**
- Please kneel, and while you're kneeling ...
- **You'll find that I move in mysterious ways.**
- You stay while I change – my vests are in the pantry and my pants are in the vestry.
- **Good Friday? I'll make it even better.**
- When you've done pulling the bells ...

IN PARLIAMENT

- Would the Right Honourable lady agree?
- **I'm Black Rod and I've got the keys to the Whips Office.**
- I have an opening for a researcher.
- **Mind if I poll you?**
- How would you like to spend an evening with a standing member?
- **I suppose losing my deposit's out of the question?**
- Would you like to come out with me, Minister?
- **Ayes to the right, noes to the left – what a pretty face.**
- Get your ermine, you've pulled.

Humph's Gazetteer
of the British Isles

NOTTINGHAM is a fine city with a fascinating history. It is well documented in official records that the city's original name was "Snottingham" or "Home of Snotts". In the 11th century, however, the new Norman rulers had difficulty pronouncing the initial letter "S", so decreed the town be called "Nottingham", and hence "Home of Notts". It's easy to understand why this change was resisted so fiercely by the people of Scunthorpe.

By far and away the best known figure with local associations is the legendary people's hero, Robin Hood. He famously, on his deathbed, shot an arrow from his trusty bow, asking that wherever in Sherwood Forest the arrow should land, there he should be laid to rest and the area covered with an enormous plastic bubble for future visitors to ride bicycles and play bingo in.

Amongst its many attractions, Nottingham proudly boasts "The Trip to Jerusalem", which is officially the oldest pub in England; a unique distinction shared with only 117 other English pubs. (By amazing coincidence, the oldest pub in Jerusalem is called "The Day Out to Centre Parcs".)

The City is associated with many famous names. The greatest bare knuckle fighter of the Victorian age was born in Nottingham, one William "Bend-E-Goes" Thompson, probably the most famous English boxer until Frank "Down-E-Goes" Bruno. Another famous fighting son of the city is Albert Ball, who shot down a total of 43 German aircraft. Mr Ball's tally would doubtless have been more, had he not been banned for life from the East Midlands Airport observation lounge in 1983. And children's author J M Barrie spent some time in Nottingham, where he was inspired to write *Peter Pan* after spotting an urchin running in the street. What a one-in-a-million chance that one should have escaped from the Marine Biology Aquarium that very day.

Nottingham has a proud tradition of commerce. Born in 1850, Jessie Boot founded the chain of chemists there that took his name. After a few years he realised his slogan: "Buy Your Drugs from Jessies" wasn't the best and so changed the company name to Boots.

BIRMINGHAM is a fine city with a fascinating history and a proud legacy of science, art and culture. Here, in the last century, William Murdoch devised gas lighting, Joseph Priestley discovered oxygen and James Watt pioneered steam power, their combined efforts producing the first British attempt at the World All-night, Underwater, Steam-roller Record. Later, of course, Priestley, Murdoch and Watt became known as one of the largest firms of estate agents in the area.

Other famous Brummies include the radical political thinker, Joseph Chamberlain, whose sons Austin and Neville also left their marks. Austin lent his name to the popular car manufactured nearby, the Chamberlain Allegro GLX, while one-time Mayor Neville Chamberlain did so much to help ensure the future restructuring of the city centre when he failed to prevent World War Two.

The town's industrial origins go back to the 14th century when peasants, finding iron ore and coal deposits, started to experiment to produce hot smelting fires and to fashion basic farm tools. It was only after decades of failure that they realised that iron doesn't burn and lumps of coal make lousy shovels. But they persevered and eventually Birmingham expanded with the Industrial Revolution.

Still little larger than a village in the 1790s, the population had grown by 1850 to nearly a quarter of a million thanks to the success of a high-quality manufacturing industry and the failure of low-quality contraception.

With the growth in production came a canal system so extensive, Birmingham is often

described as the "Venice of the North". History relates that when Canaletto was first commissioned to paint the Renaissance splendour of the Grand Canal, Venice, he crossed the Piazza San Marco, climbed the Rialto Bridge and, gazing towards the Doge's Palace, remarked "Bloody hell – it looks just like Birmingham".

STRATFORD UPON AVON is a fine city with a fascinating history most associated with the theatre. Thousands of visitors flock here from all around the world to admire the town that celebrates the career of Britain's greatest ever theatrical name by visiting Judi Dench's cottage.

Stratford is also associated with a playwright called William Shakespeare, who, it is widely believed by scholars, may have written several of Kenneth Branagh's films. Little is known about Shakespeare except that he named one of his plays after a brand of cigar – the classic love story of the young blade and his frail girlfriend: *Romeo and Slim Panatella*.

Shakespeare's birthplace is certain and many famous characters down the years have visited the very room in which he came into the world and some have even scratched their names in the glass of his window. Visitors can still make out faint signatures that include Sir Henry Irving, Mr Oscar Wilde, Miss Lily Langtree and Mr Everest Double-Glazing.

NORTHAMPTON is a fine city with a fascinating history. The town is often described as the "Naples of the Midlands", or at least as often as Naples is described as the "Northampton of Lombardy".

Originally called "Hampton" or "large village" the name "Northampton" stems from the Viking invasion, when it became "Norse Hampton". It was in 973 AD that the Saxon King Edgar regained the town from the Norse King Gudrum and freed its captive womenfolk, who were all highly impressed with his victory proclamation: "Good ladies, I have the Hampton of a Norse!".

The modern town has much to offer the intrepid Midlands tourist. But a few miles away is Rugby School, where, during a football match in 1807, a player picked up the ball and ran with it, thus creating the great English sporting tradition of being sent off for dissent after a deliberate hand-ball.

Greetings Cards

This was a round inspired by a greetings card that was specially sent into the programme. It read: "Dear *I'm Sorry I Haven't A Clue*, Get Better Soon. Yours sincerely, John Birt". The teams were asked to suggest greetings cards for previously overlooked occasions.

FOR A JAZZ MUSICIAN

To The Greatest Living English Jazz Band Leader From A Grateful Nation:
I won't write too much silly bumph,
I'd hate to embarrass dear old Humph,
There is no player of his ilk,
He's the best, Acker Bilk.

FOR A FRIEND DOWN ON HIS LUCK

Here's a card to make you cheerful,
And to wish you all the best,
Though your wife has been unfaithful,
And your home's been repossessed.

ON THE OCCASION OF SOMEONE'S CIRCUMCISION

It's the time for one small cut,
Well done on your circumcision,
I only have one tiny "but",
I think you've made the wrong decision.

FOR TIM BROOKE-TAYLOR AFTER A LEAVE OF ABSENCE FROM THE PROGRAMME

The audience are glad you're back,
Of that I'm pretty certain,
When you came on, they all stood up,
And shouted: "Where's Paul Merton?"

FOR A DOG-LOVER ON THEIR BIRTHDAY

Lovely picture of a doggy,
Spitting image of your Rover,
He'd be with you on your birthday,
If he hadn't been run over.

FOR A FRIEND WHOSE AFFAIR HAS BEEN MADE PUBLIC IN THE *NEWS OF THE WORLD*

So your paramour has kissed and told
Of you and she on pleasure bent,
This card's to say bad luck about
The mention of your measurement.

Official Sponsor

It seems that commercial advertising within the arts, entertainment and sporting media is creeping in at every level. The subliminal effect that incessant advertising can have should not be underestimated. It would seem that even our own Barry Cryer has stopped taking two bottles into the shower, preferring an entire six-pack. One doesn't have to look far to see the results that commercial sponsorship can have on some of our best-loved programmes, productions and events ...

ON TELEVISION:

- Audi They Do That?
- **Ballykissangel Delight**
- Bird's Custard Of A Feather
- **Blakes 7-Up**
- Carnation Street
- **The Cotton Buds of May**
- Eveready Steady Cook
- **The Ex-Lax Files (The Trough Is Out There)**
- ICI Claudius
- **Alan Partridge in Knowing Me B&Q**
- Kodak!
- **MFI Friday**
- News At Tennants
- **Gardener's World Of Leather**
- Newsnight Nurse
- **Prisoner Cell Block Preparation H**
- The Rock & Rolex Years
- **Some Mothercares Do 'Ave 'Em**
- Star Trex
- **They Think It's Vauxhall Nova**
- This Is Your Lifebuoy
- **Thunderbirdseye**
- The Two Rennies
- **And during Lent, the Church of England brings you The Fast Show**

AT YOUR LOCAL BOOKSHOP:

- Fisons And Lovers
- **Mr Kipling's Exceedingly Good Jungle Book**
- From the Duchess of York – Budgens The Helicopter
- **Reader's Digest presents The Complete Works of Shake**

FOR MUSIC-LOVERS:

- The Old Spice Girls
- **U2 with Boneo**
- And a concert at The Albert Hall entitled I Can't Believe It's Not Bartók.
- **Top Of The Alcopops starring Shredded Wheat Wheat Wheat**

AT THE THEATRE:

- Dancing At Lufthansa
- **Death And The Maiden Form Bra**
- A Long Day's Journey Into Night Nurse
- **No Sex Please, We're British Home Stores**
- My Fair Ladyshave
- **Five Guys Named Flymo**
- Seven Brides For 7–11
- **Starlight Express Dairies**
- Guys And Dolcis
- **Okla Homebase**
- The Andrew Lloyd Webber hits Ryvita, Phantom Of The Optrex and Dulux And His Amazing Technicolour Undercoat
- **And the Royal Shakespeare Company are putting on 'Tis Pity She's A Horlicks, Oedipus Durex (rather a safe choice), as well as a short Shakespeare Season: Burger King Lear, Big Macbeth and Spud-U-Like-It**

IN THE SPORTING ARENA:

- The FA Cup-a-Soup
- **And over at Lords, the Boots Home Pregnancy Test**

AND ON THE BIG SCREEN:

- How Green Was My Volvo
- **Debenhams Tell No Tales**
- Beverley Hill's Co-op
- **Huckleberry Findus**
- Live And Let Dynarod
- **Mothercare On Elm Street**
- Persil White And The Seven Dwarves
- **The Rymans of The Day**
- The Texas Chainstore Massacre
- **Twelve Angry Menzies**
- There's A Girl In My Superdrug
- **W H Smith Goes To Washington**
- Wall's Choc Ice Station Zebra
- **Wrigley's Top Gum**
- Whiskas Galore ... and for dogs: Pal Joey with Marrowbone Jelly
- **Alfred Hitchcock's Tesco and his other big hit, North By Nat West**

AND ON RADIO 4:

- Harpic Of The Week
- **A Rebok At Bedtime**

Universally Challenged

A version of the great college student TV quiz specially re-titled to suit the teams. It's a chance for the panellists to have their general knowledge tested with a series of questions posed by listeners. We've had quite a few queries in the postroom over the years, and our scorer, Sven, regularly works his way through them in order to pull out the hardest ones. Compare the teams' attempts with the real answers underneath ...

Q. Do animals or birds ever refer to each other by name?
A. Yes, but only if they're called Woof, Miaow or Moo.
(Ans. No, but some are able to recognise one another.)

Q. Why do the clergy wear dog collars?
A. Why does the Archbishop of Canterbury worry sheep?
(Ans. A visiting Catholic Order first wore them in the 1840s and the look caught on.)

Q. Do birds ever suffer from fear of heights?
A. Yes, that's why they flap their wings.
(Ans. There is evidence that young birds do.)

Q. Why do males of the human and related species have nipples?
A. For practice.
(Ans. Because they are genetically-defective females.)

Q. What's the best thing to do if attacked by an aggressive dog?
A. Fake an orgasm.
(Ans. You attempt to force its legs apart sideways, which tightens the ribs and causes breathing difficulties.)

Q. Do giraffes take special precautions during thunderstorms?
A. Yes, they dash down to the chemist and buy an enormous packet of three.
(Ans. No.)

Q. Is it true that the Welsh discovered America?
A. Yes, but not until 1974.
(Ans. According to Welsh legend, Madog ab Gwynedd landed in Alabama in 1169.)

Q. Is it true that cows sitting down is a portent of rain?
A. Possibly, but it's not as reliable as a pharmacy full of giraffes.
(Ans. No.)

Q. In the Book of Genesis, Adam and Eve's sons, Cain and Seth both married. Where did their wives come from?

A. The Philippines.

(Ans. They married their sisters.)

Q. Who was the Frenchman who proposed the theory that the wind is caused by trees waving their branches, and did he have any other interesting theories?

A. Yes, this was Jacques Le Converre, who had another theory that farts were caused by people saying: "Was that you?"

(Ans. It was probably a Swiss man called Jean Piaget who made various studies into "transductive reasoning". He had no other interesting theories.)

Q. How do they charm snakes?

A. They say: "You look great – have you lost skin?"

(Ans. Snake charmers don't actually charm the snakes with their flutes – snakes don't have ears. They merely annoy them.)

Q. What sport puts the greatest strain on the human body?

A. Ladies beach volleyball – half an hour of watching that and I'm absolutely knackered.

(Ans. Probably motor racing.)

Q. How do they collect caviar?

A. They send their chauffeur to pick it up for them.

(Ans. It comes from the egg sac of the Caspian Beluga Sturgeon at a price of £435 for 250 grams, or from the Norwegian Lumpfish for £4.99.)

Q. Why do bras fasten at the back?

A. If they opened at the front, she wouldn't be able to see the film properly.

(Ans. Because at one time all ladies were dressed by a maid. She must have been busy.)

Q. Do spiders have ears?

A. There was actually a famous experiment proving that spiders have ears in their legs, because if you make a loud noise a spider will run away. But if you pull its legs off ...

(Ans. They hear through the very sensitive hairs on their legs.)

Q. How did the expression "put a sock in it" originate?

A. From the instruction manual on the world's smallest tumble dryer.

(Ans. Old fashioned gramophones had no volume control so we used to put a sock in the horn. If they still banged on the walls we put in our underpants as well.)

Unhelpful Advice

Britain has a noble history of Public Information Campaigns. There were the "Coughs And Sneezes Spread Diseases" posters that first appeared in 1665, but which did little to prevent the Great Plague of London as so few bronchial rats could read. And the later warning to "Wear Something White At Night" will have been less than appreciated by anyone consequently run over by a snowplough. Here is some particularly unhelpful advice for use in certain situations.

DURING A SEX EDUCATION CLASS

- Home vasectomy can be fun
- **Now this is what happens when a bird or a bee perches on a lavatory seat**
- Think of the human body as a car: you might ask why is the ignition so near the exhaust
- **And this bit is known as the "Volvo"**
- If you're looking for a lively aphrodisiac, you cannot overdo Syrup of Figs
- **All I can say is, if you're half as good as me, you'll be great**
- The best protective is a condor, or any other large bird of prey
- **An extremely popular form of foreplay is to strike your partner on the back of the head with a euphonium**
- Now, children, size isn't everything

- **You test these things first with a pin**
- Lots of mummies and daddies practise judo in the bedroom. This can make them very hot, so the kindest thing you can do is to pour a bucket of cold water over them

WHEN VISISTING THE BRITISH MUSEUM

- On entering the Reading Room of the British Museum, it's traditional for visitors to sing the first verse of their favourite national song. If people can't hear you, they'll go: "Shh!"
- **Any of the attendants will be happy to explain to you how to play Elgin Marbles**
- The Museum has one of the largest collections of Egyptian Mummies in the world – please take one
- **A useful phrase when in the Reading Room for those whose English is no good at all is: "'Ere cock, where's the filthy stuff?"**
- Do have a look at the Rosetta Stone. You won't believe when you try it out with two or three friends just how high it bounces
- **If you'd like to demonstrate your backing for democracy, perhaps you'd like to add your signature to the Magna Carta**

WHEN VISITING MADAME TUSSAUDS

- On certain days of the year you may be asked by the staff to move about a bit: don't worry – they're stock taking
- **Kindly refrain from hanging your hats on the Chippendales exhibit**
- Interested in DIY? Why not rearrange Michael Jackson?
- **Enjoy a hilarious blindfold game of "Pin the Eyelashes on Barbara Cartland"**

WHEN VISITING CHRISTIE'S AUCTION HOUSE

- Bring your own gavel
- **It's an old English tradition to tickle the man holding the Ming**
- It's considered polite to catch the auctioneer's eye and give him a friendly nod or a wink
- **Visitors are invited to add witty captions to the Leonardo cartoons**
- When the man shouts out: "Going for the first time", you're supposed to shout back: "You do and you'll clean it up yourself!"
- **The best way to appreciate a Fabergé egg is to boil it for six minutes and then crack it open with a spoon**

Film Club

ORNITHOLOGISTS

Played while Humph took the tops off a couple of softly boiled eggs, and Sven picked up a couple of buttered soldiers ...

- The Outlaw Josey Quails
- **Nine And A Half Beaks**
- The Forbidden Gannet
- **All Quiet On The Crested Grebe**
- Sean Canary in Licensed To Trill
- **Back To The Vulture**
- There's A Gull In My Soup
- **Tern Of The Screw**
- The Maltese Ptarmigan
- **Duck Tracey**
- Moby Tit
- **Waders Of The Lost Auk**
- Anything Goose
- **The Merry Widgeon**
- Steve McQueen in Pullet
- **Hudson Hawk (that was a real turkey)**
- Oh. What A Lovely Warbler
- **Nightjar On Elm Street**
- My Left Coot
- **And anything starring Joan Collins (apparently she's seen a cockatoo).**

BISCUIT-MAKERS

Played after Samantha had nipped out for a mouthful of Jacob's ...

- Hob Nobs And Breadsticks
- **McVitie Vitie Bang Bang**
- The Singing Digestive
- **Bath Oliver Twist with the Artful Jammy Dodger**
- La Dolce Ryvita
- **Glen Garibaldi Glen Ross directed by Bicky Attenborough**
- Cream Cracker-toa East of Jaffa
- **Bring Me The Crispbread of Alfredo Garcia**
- Mutant Ginger Nut Turtles
- **The Penguin Has Landed**
- A Ryvita Runs Through It
- **Flash Bourbon**
- The Crumbs Of Navarone
- **Lord Of The Squashed Flies starring Jack Lemon Puff**
- Paint Your Wagon Wheel
- **And JRR Tolkein's The Hobnob.**

BUTCHERS

Played after Samantha had done her bit for British beef by popping off to Dewhursts (she had a lovely topside to show the teams after the show) ...

- Beef Encounter directed by David Lean
- **The Good, The Bad and the Offal**
- Butcher Cassidy and the Sundance Kidneys starring Poulet Newman and Rabbit Redford
- **Hazlitt Mince of Denmark – or the short version – Cutlet**
- Abattoir and Costello in Brawn Free
- **The Cook, The Beef, His Wife and Her Liver**
- Never Say Heifer Again
- **Pork Pie The Sailor Man**
- Little Chop Of Horrors
- **Escalope From Alcatraz**
- The Sweetbread Of York
- **Jurassic Pork**
- The Oxtail Incident
- **The Mince & The Showgirl**
- Four Weddings And A Casserole
- **Reservoir Hot Dogs**
- The Loin In Winter
- **Saturday Night Cleaver**
- Play It Again Spam
- **Rissole Down The Wind**
- Lionel Bart's Oh Liver
- **Tom Shanks in Pig and Forrest Rump**
- The Sausage Of Innocence
- **The Remains Of The Day**
- Goodbye Mr Chipolata
- **And Mrs Bobbit in Free Willy.**

Late Arrivals at. . .

THE STOCKBROKER'S BALL

- Please welcome Mr and Mrs Index and their son, Nicky Index.
- **Mr and Mrs Ding-Order and their son, Stan Ding-Order.**
- Mr and Mrs Itcrash and their son, Mark Itcrash.
- **Raise your glasses, please for the Lancashire voyeur – Phil the Looker. He's a lira.**
- Here's Nat West and his children, Pep and Tessa.
- **Mr and Mrs Ding-Rates and their debauched son, Base Len Ding-Rates.**
- Mr and Mrs Rhyming-Slang and their Futures son-in-law, Lloyd – he's a well-known banker.
- **And would you welcome, please, Mr Threadneedle-Street, his son, Fred Needle-Street, and his old lady.**
- Mr and Mrs Shore and their adopted Russian son, Stashtitov Shore.
- **Over there, our flexible friends, Dow Jones and Nikei Leeson playing Footsie. Queer as Coutts.**
- The Street-Crashes and their son, Walt Street-Crash.
- **Mr and Mrs Crates-Uppergen and their posh son, Ben Crates-Uppergen.**
- All the way from Nigeria, Mr and Mrs N'Bingley and their son, Bradford.
- **A warm welcome please for Mr and Mrs Bennett-I-Don't-Believe-These-Bank-Charges and their son, Gordon.**
- There's Hugh Nit-Trust and Ian Sider-Dealing wearing matching sweaters. Does that wool itch?
- **Mr and Mrs Owns-Index and their recently widowed mother, the Dowager Owns-Index.**

THE BUILDER'S BALL

- Will you welcome, please, Mr and Mrs Cotter-Tiling and their son, Terry Cotter-Tiling.
- **Will you welcome, please, Mr and Mrs Jay and their daughter, Iris Jay.**
- Mr and Mrs Scleavage and their daughter, Jean Scleavage.
- **Mr and Mrs Wall-Carpeting and their son, Walter Wall-Carpeting.**
- Mr and Mrs Back-On-Thursday and their son, Willoughby.
- **Mr and Mrs Bennett-That's-Twice-The-Estimate and their son, Gordon.**
- From Ireland – Brendan Beam and James Joist – as well as Con Creet and Mick Ser.
- **And also from Ireland, Mrs and Mrs O'Doors and their son, Paddy O'Doors.**
- Mrs and Mrs Antilers and their son, Rufus Antilers.
- **Mr and Mrs Loadabricks and their son, Laurie.**
- Mr and Mrs Lottle-Have-To-Be-Repainted and their son, Theo Lottle-Have-To-Be-Repainted.
- **Who is that flying in on a broomstick – it's the Thatcher.**
- Mr and Mrs Chance-Of-A-Cuppa-Tea and their son, Henny.

- **The Mendes family – including Rhoda Mendes ... she digs having her asphalt.**
- It's cabaret time. Introduced by Roy Hodd with Jasper Barrett, The Pointer Sisters and a special item, Wagner's Damntheguttering.
- **Mr and Mrs Neepot and their son, Jim Neepot.**
- It's High Society entrance now. Will you welcome the noble group Lady Foundations-First, Lord What-A-Mess and then that ubiquitous Royal libertine Filthy Prince Everywhere ... Finally, of course, Count The-Cost-Later and Baron Bank-Account.
- **Mr and Mrs Four-Sugars-In-Mine-Love and their daughter, Olive Four-Sugars-In-Mine-Love.**
- Mr and Mrs Dowframe and their daughter, Wynn

Humph's Gazetteer of the British Isles

PLYMOUTH is a fascinating city with a fine history. Now a leading port, Plymouth is first recorded in cave drawings by local Celts when they noticed an Iron Age tribe had arrived there to mine ore and smelt in a basic fashion, but to be fair this was before the invention of bathrooms.

Probably Plymouth's most celebrated son is Sir Francis Drake. Sailing for the Caribbean in 1577, Drake and his men fought their way up through a hundred leagues of the Spanish Main, ending a solid season as runners-up in Division Two. When Drake returned home in triumph the following year, the delighted townsfolk swarmed out to greet him, dancing all the way from St Andrew's Cross to the famous Plymouth Sound, an R and B derived genre not dissimilar to the later Mersey Beat.

It was from Plymouth in 1620 that the Pilgrim Fathers chose to sail. Their ship, the Mayflower, endured an eventful crossing that even saw the birth of a baby to Master and Mistress Hopkins. Inspired by the vast expanse of the Atlantic they named the boy "Oceanus Freedom Hopkins". By happy coincidence exactly the same thing happened during a commemorative voyage in 1987, and what joy there was amongst the crew at the Christening of "Oil Slick Condom Johnson".

Later, Captain Cook sailed from Plymouth for Tahiti on government service in search of the Transit of Venus. But of course those were the days when you could rely on the authorities to recover a stolen motor vehicle. After six months in the then little known *South Pacific*, Cook's crew members mutinied in protest at his constant rendition of "There Is Nothing Like A Dame".

CARDIFF (capital of Wales) is a fascinating city with a fine history. Although officially politically joined with England in 1536, the principality has preserved a unique character, thanks to a resilience born of fighting successive invasions. In turn, Romans, Saxons and Vikings were repelled by tribes banding together to terrify them with their fierce displays of close-harmony singing.

It was King Edward I who created the title and made his son "Prince of Wales", but it wasn't until this century that close ties between title and country were forged. Frequent visits between the wars by the later King Edward VIII made famous the Prince of Wales cheque, which he bounced in the Dog and Bucket, Wrexham in 1923. As King, he was forced to abdicate for his love of American divorcee Wallis Simpson. Those ignorant of the period have fallen for the myth that her first husband was called Homer. Wallis was, of course, married to Grommit.

Although the capital city of Wales only since 1955, Cardiff has many reminders of a rich 2,000-year history. Nearby is the 11th-century Castle Coch, a setting for several Hollywood movies. Filming in 1959 with Ingrid Bergman, Humphrey Bogart was inspired on a visit to a local colliery to say: "Of all the joints in all the world, you had to walk into a mine".

But a short distance from the city centre is Cardiff Arms Park, the scene of many thrilling

rugby matches. Since 1884, Wales has been a leading light in the Five Nations Cup, when the political and ethnic differences of the Irish, Scots, French and Welsh are set aside in a spirit of unity for the mutual enjoyment of stuffing it up the English.

Another event to bring top class entries to Cardiff from around the globe is the annual Singer of the World Competition, possibly the greatest international sewing-machine championship of them all.

Famous Welshmen include Owen Glendower, who gave his name to the separatist movement: "the Sons of Glendower", poet Dylan Thomas, who gave his name to the American Folk singer, Bob Thomas, and of course, Ron Davies, who gave his name to a total stranger on Clapham Common.

CHELTENHAM is a fascinating city with a fine history. Originally a small Cotswold village, this spa town first found favour during the fashionable Regency period. This was largely due to the patronage of Arthur Wellesley, the Duke of Wellington, who popularised his eponymous footwear here, Lord Sandwich who brought the leading convenience food item that bears his name and Viscount Picnic, who introduced the two. Their alfresco social gatherings were invariably also graced by Alfred Thermos, third Earl of Bovril, and Sir Jonathan-James Wasp.

Every March, race-goers gather at Cheltenham to enjoy the world-famous Gold Cup, which was originally run over hurdles by 4-year-old Arabs. Nowadays, of course, they use horses.

BATH is a fascinating town with a fine history. The city was originally called *Aquae Sulis* because of its Spa, and visitors can still see the partial remains of a system of hot and cold water pipes begun by Roman plumbing engineers in 53 AD. They returned to their depot in Verulamium in 54 AD to fetch parts and, despite a promise to return the following Thursday, have never been back since. However, they did leave the town with a unique legacy and a call-out fee of 70 quid.

Amongst other attractions is the nearby Royal Pump Room, housing a fine display of royal pumps. Next to that is the Regency Plimsoll House, just along from the Queen Anne Flip-flop archive.

Apart from the natural hot springs, intrepid tourists who seek something different might do worse than head for the Norwegian quarter of the town, with its many ethnic bistros serving traditional Scandinavian cuisine. After enjoying a dinner of wild elk and smorgasbord, washed down with pewter goblets of whale blubber mead, they may care to wander by the river and help celebrate the Festival of the Burning Longship, when fierce, bearded locals don horned helmets and wave mighty battle swords as they chant in praise of their Lord of Valhalla. Anyone who visits Bath and misses this colourful and dramatic event will kick themselves when they realise they should have gone to Reykjavik.

Missed Hits

Some otherwise first-rate films, plays, songs and TV programmes have sunk without trace for want of a decent title. Humph asked the teams to come up with some interesting suggestions for him, and having done that, suggest some titles of sure-fire flops ...

- **Cyrano de Basingstoke**
- Indiana Jones and the VAT Returns
- **Edward Fingerhands**
- Kiss of the Ciderwoman
- **Batman Returns – The Video**
- Godzilla Versus Petula Clark – This Time It's Personal
- **When Harry Met Janet Street-Porter**
- Seven Dwarves For Seven Samurai
- **Sleepless In Sheffield**
- Give My Regards To Broadmoor
- **The Lada In Red**
- Natural Born Grocers
- **Big Knobs And Broomsticks**
- Gonorrhoea With The Wind
- **Shallow Gravy**
- Cheltenham Prefers Blondes
- **The Guns Of Neasden**
- Jeffrey Bernard Is Fit And Well
- **Piddler On The Roof**
- Annie Get Your Gin
- **The Sound Of Mucus**
- Spot (the failed Grease)
- **Bernard Manning And Friends – A One Man Show**
- My Old Man's A Waste Disposal Operative
- **Man Dogs And Belgians**
- It's A Hap Hap Rainy Day
- **Knees Up Gordon Brown**
- Meet Me In St Leonards
- **The Sound Of Silage**
- Oh, What A Beautiful Awning
- **A Nightingale Sang In Barclays Bank**
- The Sun Has Got His Pants On
- **Trouble Over Bridgwater**
- People Will Say We're In Hove
- **Ah Bidets Are Here Again**
- The Wizard Of Ongar
- **Twenty-four Hours from Tulse Hill**
- Robin Cook, Robin Cook, Riding Through The Glen
- **Bruce Forsyth's Generation Gap**
- Cagney And Lassie
- **The Benson & Hedges World Smoker Championship**
- Deaf Date
- **Dodo Watch**
- Tales Of The Expected

Jargon

BUILDER'S JARGON

- **This needs pointing.**
  This needs pointing the other way.
- **We could start Monday.**
  Pick any Monday and you'd be wrong.
- **Make good.**
  Disguise cock-up.
- **A quotation.**
  One eighth of the final price.
- **You'll notice there are a few differences from the drawings.**
  We had the plans upside-down.
- **Oh, we do electrics.**
  No, we don't.
- **Pebbledash.**
  Throw a stone through the window and run off.
- **That door won't stick when the wood's dried out.**
  That door won't open when the wood's dried out.
- **It'll be a feature.**
  It'll be an eyesore.
- **Oh, we do plumbing.**
  No, we don't.
- **African Orange would suit this room.**
  I've got a whole bucket-load of it in my van.
- **Don't you worry, you won't know we're there.**
  They won't be there.

RESTAURANT JARGON

- **Soup of the Day.**
  The day was March 14th, 1943.
- **Dawn-picked mushrooms.**
  We don't actually know when Dawn picked the mushrooms.
- **Good evening sir, my name is André.**
  My name is Neville and I was raised in Catford.
- **Chef's Special.**
  No, he's not.
- **Help yourself to as much salad as you like.**
  We have tiny salad plates.
- **Nestling in a bed of lettuce.**
  The cockroaches are mating.
- **Would you like a drink at the bar first?**
  Your table isn't ready, please give us a lot of money while you're waiting for it.
- **Which wine did you say again, sir?**
  I'm going to pretend I didn't understand your French accent just to embarrass you in front of your friends.
- **Service is not included.**
  Service is not included.
- **Chef has asked me to say that he particularly recommends the turbot.**
  If we don't shift that turbot by tonight, we'll have to throw it out.

ESTATE AGENTS' JARGON

- **No chain involved.**
  The toilet doesn't flush.
- **Ten minutes from the sea.**
  Or even less if the cliff crumbles.
- **Suit elderly couple.**
  Smells of cabbage.
- **A1 condition.**
  The A1 runs through the garden.
- **Under offer.**
  Gazumping in progress.
- **Ideal for first time buyer.**
  Can only be sold to people who don't
  know what a real house is supposed
  to look like.
- **Imposing.**
  The neighbours will come round
  and never leave.
- **Utility room.**
  A toilet with a washing machine in it.
- **Bedroom floor of finest wood.**
  One heavy footstep and you'll all go
  down to breakfast together.
- **Ready for immediate occupation.**
  It's in Jersey and the owners were
  collaborators during the War.
- **Compact garden.**
  Access to windowbox.
- **Semi detached.**
  It's falling apart.
- **Listed building.**
  The Tower of Pisa.

BANKERS' JARGON

- **Working weekdays.**
  We knock off at 3.30.
- **Your balance.**
  Tipped in our favour.
- **How may I help you?**
  Go ahead punk, make my day!
- **Current accounts.**
  Tales from the river bank.
- **Your PIN number will be sent
  later.**
  We're still working on a number you'll
  never remember.
- **The Listening Bank.**
  What?
- **The Bank That Likes To Say Yes.**
  Piss off.
- **Index-linked.**
  Stuck to my finger.
- **Can you borrow £10,000?**
  Can you borrow £10,000? You can
  borrow £10,000 if you're a fat crook
  with Mafia connections or President of a
  South American dictatorship.
- **Mr Jolly, your manager, has taken
  early retirement.**
  Mr Jolly is fed up with having to check
  everything with Head Office and not use
  his discretion based on local knowledge
  built up over many years and is to be
  replaced by a 9-year-old with no
  powers whatsoever.

Historical Headlines

A popular round where the teams suggest how certain historical events might be reported in today's newspapers and periodicals. It's similar to an old game called "Historical Headlice", where the teams were presented with four specimens of parasitic insect and had to place them in correct order of succession to the Hapsburg throne ...

JESUS CHRIST BORN IN STABLE

- The Daily Mail: Branson Sponsors Virgin Birth
- **The Guardian: Baby Born In Mangle**
- The Daily Express: "We'll Call Him David" Say Mr And Mrs Icke
- **The Times: "We Were Following Yonder Star" – Unlikely Claim By Three Wise Men Held At Customs**
- The Independent: Sparse Queues For Herod's Christmas Sale
- **The Sun: Jezza Of Nazza Born In Bezza – Gazza In Gaza**
- The Mirror: You Wait Ages For A Wise Man And Then Three Turn Up At Once
- **Knitting & Knitters: Special Swaddling Supplement**
- The Guardian: Corrections & Clarifications: In our earlier edition "Son of Dog" should have read "Ackrington Stanley"
- **Exchange & Mart: Unwanted Frankincense And Myrrh. Will Swap For Nintendo**

THE GREAT FIRE OF LONDON

- The Daily Telegraph: French Farmers Protest Reaches London
- **The Financial Times: Capital Goes Up**
- The Guardian: London's Burping – Police Suspect Arse
- **The Scotsman: Tee Hee Hee!**
- The Star: Phew, What A Scorcher!
- **Yorkshire Evening Post: Leeds Man Singed**
- Insurance Weekly: Oh, Bugger!
- **The Radio Times: TV Chief Says Great Idea For A Series**
- The Sport: Elvis Seen In Pudding Lane
- **The Guardian – Corrections & Clarifications page: Yesterday's headline "Paula To Be Reconstructed By Sir Christopher Wren" should have read "St Paul's To Be Reconstructed By Christ Knows When"**
- The Lancet: Plague Cure A Success

ROBIN HOOD WINS NOTTINGHAM ARCHERY CONTEST

- **The Express: Tournament Starts 15 Minutes Late – Outrage As Archers Move To Two O'clock**
- Lincoln Green 'Un: Robin Hood Makes Meal Of Victory In This Year's Eaten An Arrow Match
- **The Telegraph: Reverend Spooner Arrested In Friar Tuck Incident**
- The Nottingham Clarion: Council Install Little John In Forest
- **The Guardian – Corrections & Clarifications page: Robin Hood's partner Friar Tuck has "passed a late fitness test" and not "pissed a late fatness test"**

THE DEATH OF HAMLET PRINCE OF DENMARK

- The Telegraph: Danish Blood Bath – No Britons Hurt
- **The Dog Breeders Gazette: Great Dane Puts Self Down**
- The Times: Blair Says Whittling Down Of Royal Family A Success
- **The Stage: Touring Players Unexpectedly Available For Panto**
- The Times Comment: Just Be!
- **The Star: You Don't Know Your Arras From Your Elbow**
- The Guardian – Corrections & Clarifications page: Yesterday's headline "Laughter At Elsinore" should have read "Slaughter At Erinsborough"

Complete Proverbs

It's a regrettable failing of the education system that the youth of today can't tell the difference between a proverb, a metaphor and a simile. They'll certainly find themselves sailing close to thin ice like a red flag in a china shop barking up the wrong end of the stick if they don't pull their trousers up. Here are the results of a round called "Complete Quotes". It was based on an old parlour game called "Incomplete Sentences", first popularised by a Mr Ernest Saunders.

- **Many hands make ...**
  a lot of fingers.
- **When in Rome do ...**
  what the Mafia tells you.
- **You can't make a silk purse out of ...**
  an old washing-up liquid bottle.
- **A fool and his money ...**
  are welcome at Lloyds.
- **If the cap fits ...**
  better safe than sorry.
- **A little learning is a ...**
  new educational policy.
- **Ask no questions and you'll be told ...**
  ... well, nothing really.
- **Pride comes before ...**
  of lions.
- **Blood is thicker than ...**
  Kaliber.
- **A swarm of bees in May is worth a load of hay, but a swarm in July ...**
  isn't.
- **Cleanliness is next to ...**
  impossible.

- **One swallow doesn't make ...**
  an orgy.
- **There's no smoke without ...**
  flatulence.
- **Give a thief enough rope and he'll ...**
  run off with it.
- **When the cat's away, the mice will**
  ... use the flap.
- **If you can't beat 'em ...**
  what's the point of teaching?
- **Hell hath no fury like ...**
  Mrs Bradley of 43 The Glebe, Orpington.
- **In for a penny ...**
  and don't forget to wash your hands afterwards.
- **Once bitten ...**
  twice licked – that's enough foreplay.
- **The way to a man's heart is through his ...**
  chest cavity with a chain saw.
- **The Devil finds work for ...**
  Andi Peters.
- **It's an ill wind that blows ...**
  ... but the silent ones are the worst.

- **What goes up ...**
  must be your decision, Myrtle.
- **If you want a thing done well ...**
  leave it in the microwave overnight.
- **It's a long road ...**
  that has no gents.
- **Out of the mouths of babes and sucklings ...**
  and straight down the back of your suit.
- **It is easier for a camel to pass through the eye of a needle ...**
  if you've put it through the liquidiser first.
- **In the land of the blind, the one-eyed man ...**
  doesn't have to bother too much about his appearance.
- **Neither a borrower nor a lender be**
  ... Be an accountant.
- **There's many a slip twixt ...**
  wicket keeper and gully.
- **You can't teach an old dog new ...**
  clear physics.
- **You can lead a horse to water, but you can't make it ...**
  scuba dive.
- **Give a man a fish and you feed him for a day; teach a man to fish ...**
  and you have a 12-part series, a book and two or three videos.
- **Birds of a feather ...**
  is a crap television programme.
- **Some men have only one book in them, others ...**
  don't indulge in that practice.
- **See no evil, hear no evil ...**
  your television's exploded.
- **See a pin and pick it up, all day long you'll have ...**
  a pin.
- **Don't try to run before you can ...**
  pull up your trousers.
- **He who sups with the Devil has need of a long ...**
  after-dinner speech.
- **The early bird catches the ...**
  5.45 to Paddington.
- **Too many cooks ...**
  on television.
- **Red sky at night, shepherd's delight ...**
  red light at night, Shepherd's Market.
- **Don't count your chickens ...**
  out loud as it excites the other patients.
- **What you lose on the swings ...**
  is what you had in the Indian restaurant before you got on the swings.
- **Don't get your knickers in ...**
  a car boot sale.
- **Don't let the sun go down on your ...**
  newspaper order.
- **Fools rush in ...**
  the minute MacDonalds opens.

Songbook

FISHERMEN

The team were asked to suggest suitable songs for fishermen during a trip to Plymouth. Needless to say. Samantha had already nipped out to enjoy a portion of local winkles in cider ...

- The theme from The Anchovy and The Ecstasy
- **I Who Have Netting by Jacques Brill**
- Where Did You Get That Trout?
- **A whole album of Sole music sung by Pike and Tuna Turbot, Ray Charles and Little Pilchard**
- Happy Dace Are Here Again
- **Fish Finger by Shirley Bass**
- If I'd Known You Were Coming I'd Have Baked A Hake
- **Why Are We Whiting?**
- We're All Going On A Summer Halibut
- **Three Steps To Herring**
- Kiss Me Skate
- **I Took My Carp To A Party**
- Salmon Chanted Evening
- **Stickleback Writer**
- Message In A Bottle-Nose Whale by Sting Ray
- **Prawn Free**
- Sturgeon On The Corner Watching All The Girls Go By
- **Cod Save Our Gracious Bream**

- I'm Leaning On A Lamprey
- **How Much Is That Dogfish In The Window?**
- Shark! The Herald Angels Sing
- **Bream Bream Bream**
- And The Bait Goes On
- **Whale Meat Again**
- Rod Stewart singing Maggot May
- **Oh I Do Like To Be Beside The Coelacanth**
- Hake Rattle And Rollmops
- **Girls Just Want To Have Fins**
- Nellie The Halibut Packed Her Trunk

CRIMINALS

Played while Samantha had popped off to the Old Bailey to help try some suspects who'd been brought to justice by the Police. (She said there was nothing more satisfying than seeing hardened ones being put away by the Yard...)

- Who Were You With Last Night?
- **Theme from You've Been Framed**
- 'Allo 'Allo, Whose Your Shady Friend?
- **Wouldn't It Be Robbery?**
- Morning Has Been Broken Into by Cat Burglar Stevens
- **Smash Grab Wallop What A Picture by Tommy Steal**
- Twenty Tiny Fingers by the Artist Formerly Known as Prints
- **Parole Over Beethoven**
- Safe Blowin' In The Wind by Bob Villain
- **Please Release Me**
- Don't Go Breaking And Entering
- **Blinded By The Light (On Top Of The Police Car) by Manfred Manslaughter**
- Ram-a-raid-a-ding-dong
- **I Dismember You**
- Here Comes The Bribe
- **Rock Around The Dock**
- And of course, Superintendanttellsoldlag hisalibisatrocious

COMPUTER PROGRAMMERS

Played after Samantha had nipped out to meet a nice chap who was training her in computer skills. She was hoping he'd show her the three and a half inch floppy he'd got in his Mac...

- The Mouse Of The Rising Sun
- **Querty Querty Chip Chip**
- The Nerdy Song
- **With Love From VDU**
- Thanks For The 38K Random Access Memory
- **Thoroughly Modem Millie**
- Floppy Discs Are Here Again
- **When I'm Cleaning Windows**
- When I'm Cleaning Windows 95
- **Da Doo ROM ROM**
- Another One Megabytes The Dust
- **Please Release Key**
- I'm Forever Blowing Bubblejets
- **Tulips From Amstrad Damn**
- CD ROM and MS DOS And Little Lambsie Divie
- **Superhighwayfragilistic-applemacintosis**
- Some Day My Printer Will Work
- **IT For Two**
- Internet The Arches
- **Our Mouse Is A Very Very Very Nice Mouse by Mouse Mat Monro.**

Humph's Gazetteer
of the British Isles

GLASGOW There is a fascinating history attached to this fine Scottish city. Founded in the year 550 AD by St Mungo, life over several centuries centred around its "Kirk" for a people known as the "Scottie", later joined by the "Sulu", the "Uhura" and the "More Power Mr Chekovs". And it was their occasional explorations South to face the encroaching English that led to the first recorded use of the line: "It's civilisation Jimmy, but not as we know it".

The city grew steadily and by the 18th century was Britain's major port for trade with the New World. Sadly, rapid decline followed the American War of Independence, when the Revolutionary Colonists and their Native Indian allies fought the British Redcoats to throw off the oppression of awful holiday camp comedians.

But the city recovered with the Industrial Revolution and through the 19th century embraced the Age of Steam. Today, nostalgic Glasgwegians pay good money to spend whole days enjoying the static display of Victorian rolling stock known as Virgin Rail.

Glasgow's most famous son in the field of art and design is surely Charles Rennie Mackintosh, whose family also lent their name to the popular waterproof garment. Sadly, a simple confusion over Rennie and Mackintosh led to many braving inclement weather wearing nothing but an indigestion tablet.

EDINBURGH There is a fascinating history attached to this fine Scottish capital. Now the seat of the recently devolved Scottish Parliament, the Scots voted finally to split from the Union because the English notion of having a good time is to visit Edinburgh in August to watch a Hungarian juggle live lobsters in a street full of Americans while paying over the odds for a Mars Bar deep-fried in batter.

But apart from the annual Festival, the city boasts many cultural and academic achievements. It is the birthplace of an education system that is the envy of Britain,

enjoying what many south of the border may think is an amazingly highlight racy rat, but is in fact an amazingly high literacy rate. Despite this, only three Scottish language expressions are in regular usage in England: "Kilt", "Haggis" and "Partick Thistle Nil".

The list of members of the new Parliament makes fascinating reading – a veritable "Who's That?" of British politics. However, one of the better known champions for the cause of Scottish independence is actor Sean Connery. Indeed, such is his enthusiasm for his mother country that Connery makes a highly principled stand in his movies by refusing to use any other accent, no matter what the role.

NEWCASTLE upon TYNE There is a fascinating history attached to this fine city situated conveniently near Scotland in this book. A fortified settlement was established here in Roman times by Hadrian, the regional consul who became famous for the building of Roman Walls; in fact, by the end of his lifetime they became one of the largest ice-cream suppliers of the 3rd century.

In the Saxon period the town was known as "Monk Chester", because of the large number of monks here, but was subsequently occupied by marauding vikings, when it became known as "Danish Gitchester". But the city took its modern name when the old city ramparts were replaced by a "new castle", built by Robert Curthose, the bastard son of William the Conqueror. He wasn't, in fact, illegitimate. That's just what customers called him when they saw his shoddy building work.

Newcastle also proudly boasts the birthplace of the electric light bulb, the gas turbine and the steam locomotive, and it was here that the Industrial Revolution reached its peak with the first successful demonstration of Stevenson's Rocket, following the earlier disappointment when Stevenson's Milk Bottle fell over.

As the main seaport linking England with Scandinavia, Captain Scott sailed from here to train for his polar expedition. Returning some months later in anticipation of a warm and passionate greeting from his young fiancée, one can only imagine his dismay on finding a Norwegian had got there first.

That the English language has been greatly enriched by the Far North of Britain is witnessed by the many phrases it has evolved to denote a pointless activity. It's because Newcastle was the country's biggest exporter of coal, neighbouring Durham sent most of her young men to train in the shoemaking trade, and Edinburgh in the summer months becomes filled to bust with English and American tourists, that we now enjoy the expressions "Coals to Newcastle", "Cobblers to Durham" and "Arseholes to Edinburgh".

Out To Lunch

How often have you wished for a game based on the messages people pin to their doors at lunchtime? No, neither have I ...

- **Nicholas Soames:**
  Gone to lunch. Back in April.

- **Melinda Messenger:**
  Just popped out.

- **Peter Tatchell:**
  I'm Out.

- **Kate Moss:**
  Gone to lunch – back now, actually.

- **The Queen:**
  Gone to launch.

- **Apathy Society:**
  Maybe we won't come back at all.

- **Mike Atherton:**
  I won't be long.

- **John McCrirrick:**
  Gone To Lunch. Back Naughty Boy At Haydock Park.

- **Quasimodo:**
  Out to hunch.

- **Barbara Cartland:**
  Completely out to lunch.

- **General Custer:**
  Me and the lads have popped out for an Indian.

- **Captain Oates:**
  I've gone out. I may be some time.

- **Bertrand Russell:**
  I'm not here at the moment, and yet perhaps I am in a very real sense, like the page of a book before you've turned it over: Is it printed? Is it blank? So I may well be here, but why are we here, particularly when we're not?

Sound Charades

A variation of the popular parlour game, where teams take it in turns to enact the title of a book, film or TV programme for their opponents to guess. In our version, the teams are permitted the use of their mouths, in a process known technically as "speaking". We recently experimented with a similar game called "Smell Charades", but were forced to evacuate the studio after Barry did "Animal Farm". And an attempt to do "Feel Charades" was abandoned after Tim tried to do "Lady Chatterley's Lover" and we had to call the police. Here are some examples to try on your friends at home ...

BOOK AND FILM – TWO WORDS

DOUGAL: Ah. Hamish.

HAMISH: Ah. Dougal.

DOUGAL: You'll have had your tea.

HAMISH: Indeed I have. But tell me now, what's that peeping out of your sporran?

DOUGAL: What? Oh that! That's my Ning.

HAMISH: You'd tell your grandchildren about a thing like this. I've never seen a Ning before. Get it out and give us a proper look.

DOUGAL: Easier said than done. Dougal.

HAMISH: Why's that?

DOUGAL: Well, your Ning isn't much of a one for company.

HAMISH: You mean he's easily embarrassed?

DOUGAL: Oh very, very. Keeps himself to himself, you know. Look! Look, you can see him going a funny colour.

HAMISH: Oh, I see. You mean he's not comfortable with strangers?

DOUGAL: No, no he isn't. And that's why he's called ...

(The Shining)

TV PROGRAMME –
THREE LETTERS

EADIE: I want some scratch cards.

ETHEL: Eadie, be patient. Join that line of people.

EADIE: How am I gonna get my scratch cards?

ETHEL: Go and stand behind that person ever there, Eadie.

EADIE: What do I do? I'm 84, you know.

ETHEL: Stand in the line. How else can I put it?

(QED)

FILM – THREE WORDS

VOICE 1: Would you like some more, Field Marshall?

VOICE 2: No thank you, I've had quite enough.

(The Full Monty)

TV PROGRAMME –
THREE WORDS

BOY: 'Ere, Dad. The kids at school say that your sister Muriel played for Arsenal.

DAD: Well, they're right, Gavin. She did indeed play for Arsenal.

BOY: I can't believe that, Dad.

DAD: It may be hard to believe, but let me prove it to you. Have a look at what I've got here in this drawer ... Look at these.

BOY: Gosh!

DAD: Yes, they're strong, you see – reinforced gusset, a go-faster flap and a little Arsenal logo on the leg.

BOY: What's a gusset, Dad?

DAD: He's a rugby player, I believe.

(Auntie's Sporting Bloomers)

 **Postbag**

ON THE JOYS OF ENGLISH PASTIMES:

Dear Melvyn,

Ipswich 2, Norwich 47. That's my favourite road sign. What's yours?

Yours faithfully,

Mrs Trellis,

North Wales

ON THE RETURN OF A MUCH-MISSED PANELLIST:

Dear Ulrika,

So pleased to hear that Tim Brooke-Taylor is back. With him away, the show was like *Hamlet* without the balcony scene.

Yours sincerely,

Mrs Trellis,

North Wales

ON TAKING UP BIRDWATCHING:

Dear Vanessa,

Tits like coconuts!

However, sparrows prefer breadcrumbs.

Yours faithfully,

Mrs Trellis,

North Wales

ON THE PUBLICATION OF THE "I'M SORRY I HAVEN'T A CLUE" OFFICIAL LIMERICK BOOK:

Dear Mrs Antrobus,

Hats off to the boys! Their book of limericks is a great read at under a tenner and published by Orion! It inspired me to try writing a limerick myself, which I would love one day to hear read out loud on your show.

> There was a young lady from Slough
> Who developed a very bad cough
> She wasn't to know
> It would last until now
> Let's hope the poor girl will through.

Yours truly,

Mrs Trellis,

North Wales

FROM A DEVOTED FAN:

Dear Nicholas,

How about some signed photographs?

Yours faithfully,

Mrs Trellis,

North Wales

(Editor's note: Thank you, Mrs Trellis. The photos were very nice.)

A SHORT POSTCARD FROM THE HOLIDAY RESORT OF RHYL:

Dear ...

Having a lovely ...

Weather not so ...

Wish you were ...

Yours ...

Mrs ...

(PS Due to power cut in hotel last night, had to write this under lighthouse.)

Madrigals

A Midsummer Night's Madrigal

arr. Sell

I joined a band of stroll-ing players, 'Twas on-ly for a lark. We played A Mid-sum-mer Night's Dream In leaf-y Reg-ent's Park. I gave my Bot-tom night-ly, Though my Bot-tom's past its peak. I did it in the op-en air My case comes up next week.

THE HUMPHREY LYTTELTON MADRIGAL

As I walked out one evening
To a Humphrey Lyttelton gig
I knew I'd come to the wrong place
For the audience was quite big
So I went round to the Gents next door
Downcast and sad at heart
And there stood Humph with his horn in his hand
He said: "Thank God, now we can start".

COSTA BRAVA MADRIGAL

When I reached the Costa Brava
I was high on Duty Free
A lusty Spaniard came along
As I paddled in the sea
I said: "You have the finest beach
I ever saw in my life."
He grabbed my castanets
And said: "That's no beach, that's my wife."

A PRESIDENT CLINTON MADRIGAL

As I walked out one May morning
All in the White House grounds
From out the Oval Office
I heard such curious sounds
I peeped in through the window
And saw Bill standing on a bucket
I said: "What are you doing?"
He said: "I'm trying to see Nantucket"

The President then asked me:
"Have you seen my White House staff?"
I misconstrued his meaning
And I gave a nervous laugh.
Then up there popped a fine young lass
He said: "This is my lodger"
I said: "What is that in her mouth?"
He said: "A jammy dodger".

What Is The Question?

This game should not be confused with the amusing party game played by French philosophers entitled: "What Is A Question?" Nor indeed should it be confused with their other favourites: "I Spy Therefore I Am", "Deconstruct The Parcel" and "Pin The Tail On The Externalised Image Of The Long-Eared Quadruped". You can easily play along at home. Simply study the answers below and then, like the teams, try to imagine what the original question might have been ...

A. Hanging in the bathroom
Q. What is too good for people who pee in the bath?
(Real question: Where did Francis I of France keep the Mona Lisa when he originally bought it in 1517?)

A. 90% of it is done by females
Q. What do men like about housework?
(Real question: How does a pride of lions share out the hunting responsibilities?)

A. Not if your name is Mary
Q. Is Christmas a good name?
(Real question: Is it legal to be a prostitute in Sienna?)

A. It always comes back
Q. What's the worse thing about being sick out of a train window?
(Real question: What is the most remarkable thing about Last Of The Summer Wine*?)*

A. They have both sets of sexual organs on their bodies
Q. What singles out a successful Eurovision song contest winner?
(Real question: How can you tell that worms are hermaphrodite?)

A. They weren't allowed to touch his face
Q. What were Robin Cook's plastic surgeons not allowed to do?
(Real question: What part of Emperor Napoleon's body were prostitutes forbidden to touch?)

A. Two in the bush
Q. What was the nickname of the legendary Norse folk hero Tuin, who had an enormous beard?
(Real question: What is one in the hand better than?)

A. Divine Brown
Q. Och aye, how was it for you, your
Majesty?
(Real question: Who got Hugh Grant's
picture on the front of the papers?)

A. Chocks away!
Q. Where is Mr Chock?
(Real question: What was Biggles'
catchphrase?)

A. Hairy, slimy, bloody, oily and smelly
Q. Name the cast in Quentin Tarrantino's
Snow White
(Real question: Name five adjectives ending
in "y" that have all been used to describe
Lord Archer)

**A. A creature halfway between a man
and a horse**
Q. What is a saddle?
(Real question: What is a centaur?)

A. A royal flush
Q. What follows the royal we?
(Real question: What beats a straight flush
in poker?)

A. Pensioners and buns
Q. Name two things you can often see in a
Post Office if you take some buns
(Real question: What is Chelsea famous for?)

A. They both change colour
Q. What do Judith Chalmers and Michael
Jackson have in common?
(Real question: What connects chameleons
and traffic lights?)

A. Saltpetre
Q. Jesus, what do you want on your last
supper?
(Real question: What is added to charcoal
and sulphur to make gunpowder?)

A. Seven hundred wives
Q. Who can do the work of 4 million men?
(Real question: How many wives did King
Solomon have?)

**A. Fully extend the right arm and
move it up and down a few times**
Q. Before heading off for work in the
morning, what exercise does a farm vet do?
(Real question: How would you demonstrate
the slowing down arm signal during your
driving test?)

A. In and out fifteen hundred times
Q. What is an average day like in a farm
vet's life?
(Real question: What does the cox of the
winning crew say during the boat race?)

New Versions

As regular listeners to the programme will be only too aware, Humph is always keen to keep up with modern innovations. Only recently he had his old PC upgraded to a detective inspector. Here are some of the teams' attempts to render certain much repeated old stories or events in fresh and challenging new styles ...

WORLD WAR II IN THE STYLE OF A PARISH MAGAZINE

Last Saturday Mr Chamberlain, reading from a piece of paper, introduced Mr Hitler, who kindly opened the proceedings with an amusing speech and an impromptu invasion of Poland. Later, Mr Churchill, standing in for Mr Chamberlain, organised some games on the beaches, and was particularly fulsome in his praise of the few who took part in the aerial display. The W.I. as usual did a splendid job feeding 50 million, and their spam stall was a great success. Winners included Dame Myra Hess (dried egg and spoon race), Charles de Gaulle (potato most like its owner) and Mussolini (silliest walk). As usual, everyone sat on the greasy poles. Mention should be made of some Americans who appeared later in the afternoon to help clear up. The vicar finally thanked everyone for taking part and fervently hoped this event would not take place ever again.

THE BEHEADING OF CHARLES I IN THE STYLE OF AN AGONY AUNT

Dear Charles I,

It is of course so easy to be wise after the event, though given the event, in your case the reverse is probably true. When the head is severed from the body, wisdom tends to go straight out of the window. How sensible of you though to take my advice and wear three shirts. It was foolish of you however to ignore my best suggestion – not to turn up. So you were pig-ignorant before and during the event, and even more so afterwards. But then again you have a descendant of the same name who talks to lupins and is constantly writing to me. What a family.

Love,

Auntie Will

THE FIRE OF LONDON IN THE STYLE OF A RADIO 4 ANNOUNCER

Well now, before the next programme, here is a road traffic report. The fire which started late last night in Pudding Lane is still out of control and now covers most of the city of London ... And speaking of the city, you can hear an extended version of *Money Box* with Louise Botting and Vincent Duggleby at 11.30 on Monday morning. With thousands of Londoners fleeing from the blaze, the roads leading out of the city are at a standstill, with tailbacks stretching right out to the Hangar Lane gyratory system ... Well, St Paul's cathedral may have gone up in smoke, but there are some glum faces at *Brookfield Farm*...

THE GUNPOWDER PLOT IN THE STYLE OF RAYMOND CHANDLER

She stood in the middle of the office, wide hat, shades, some sort of cloak. She had great legs, all I could see of them from the knees down. "Here's looking at you, kid" I said. "Who are you?" "Guy Fawkes," she said. Her beard moved up and down like voles mating. "You, Marlowe?" "I'm Marlow," I said. "God, Dr Faustus is boring," she said. I lit up a cigarette. "Don't do that!" she said, "I'm a living bomb" "You can say that again, baby," I said. She walked slowly to the window. "I'm going to blow up the Houses of Parliament," she said. "Well," I said, "they can't hang, draw and quarter you for that". But they did.

Late Arrivals at ...

THE CAR ENTHUSIASTS' BALL

- Pray silence, thrust yourself under the vehicle and lay prostrate as approaching us through the garage come Mr and Mrs Cap and their son, Herb Cap.
- **Mr and Mrs Screen-Wipers and their daughter, Wynn.**
- Will you welcome Mr and Mrs Buretta and their son, Karl Buretta.
- **From India, an alligator wrestler, D I Singh and his Hindi Gaitor, introduced by D Frost.**
- Also from Spain, Manuel Gears with his friend, Taco Graph.
- **Mr and Mrs Dependable and their son, reliant Robin.**
- There's Mr and Mrs Petrol-Again and their daughter, Renata Petrol-Again.
- **Mr and Mrs Trelease-Knob and their daughter, Bonnie Trelease-Knob.**
- Mr and Mrs Gin-Failure and their rather posh son, Ian Gin-Failure.
- **From France, the Absorbers and their son, Jacques.**
- Mr and Mrs Costyer and their ex-military son, Gunner Costyer.
- **Give a nice German welcome and say Audi to Thor Sprung and Dirk Technic.**
- It's cabaret time with Birley Chassis singing "Big Suspension" and Diesel Kneisel, who's going to jump Leeds.
- **From Spain via Sweden, it's Mr and Mrs Go-Atstarting-Itagain and their son, Juan Lars Go-Atstarting-Itagain.**
- Mr and Mrs Tatious-Vehicles and their son, Austin.
- **Who's that lovely lady over there? Cor! Tina!**
- Mr and Mrs Erup-Withfourstar and their son, Phil.
- **Mr and Mrs System and their unbelieving daughter – that's Di Agnostic System – and the very believing Rev Counter.**
- There's Mr Tee and his son, Mo ... And he's brought his incontinent dog, 3.5-litre Rover.
- **And alarming news – a plane has recently shed its load of old car parts ... it's been raining Datsun cogs.**
- Mr and Mrs Perlitre and their son, Miles Perlitre.
- **And will you welcome Mr and Mrs Le Jague and their daughter, Dame Le Jague.**

THE MORTICIANS' BALL

- As always, the first to arrive, it's premature Beryl.
- **Would you welcome first a party here from the Wild West (Derge City to be precise): Hearse Cartwright, Gene Mortuary and Roy Rogers with his horse, Trigger Mortis.**
- And will you welcome a spluttering gentleman from Wales, Dai Thedeath, who appears to be having a coffin fit.
- **And Mr and Mrs Stone with their son, Ed Stone.**
- From Scotland, the crazy stone-carver, Monumental Mason.
- **Mr and Mrs Stover and their father, Pa Stover.**
- Also, Mr and Mrs Vault, and their agricultural son, Farmer Lee Vault.
- **Daddy and Mummy Fied.**
- From the West Country, Eliza Body.
- **Welcome the Gee sisters, Ella Gee and Ula Gee.**
- From Australia, welcome the grave-faced, Digger Pitt.
- **Mr and Mrs Beloved and their daughter, Dilly Beloved.**
- Unroll the black carpet and wave your plumage for Mr and Mrs Mortis and their dyslexic son, Roger.
- **From Mexico, Signor and Signore Dropadabox and their daughter, Donna Dropadabox.**
- Mr and Mrs Mason and their huge son, Monumental Mason.
- **Raise those lovely black top hats, for here come Mr and Mrs Reaper and their son, Graham Reaper … and, in fact, he's brought his whore, Topsy.**
- From Wales, Mr and Mrs Jones and their cheerful son, Happy Taff.
- **Mr and Mrs Balming-Fluid and their daughter, Emma.**
- Lord Reith, accompanied by Earl Fire and Dame Nation.
- **Mr and Mrs Missed and their mournful son, Sad Lee Missed.**
- And finally, from Sweden, Lars Rights and Lars Post.
- **Enjoy the cabaret: Tom Jones singing "The Last Vaults".**

Humph's Gazetteer
of the British Isles

SOUTHSEA is often overlooked in favour of its more famous neighbour, PORTSMOUTH, but as Portsmouth is a lively, bustling city dripping with a rich history, that comes as no surprise. The great pioneering civil engineer, Isambard Kingdom Brunel, was born here and christened in the local church amid great celebration, as his parents had just won the first two prizes in Southsea's "most stupid novelty name for a small child" competition.

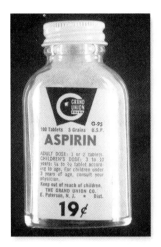

Later in Victorian times, Sir Arthur Conan Doyle was practising in Southsea as a young GP when he wrote his very first Sherlock Holmes novel "The Curse of the Black Hand", subtitled "Take Two Aspirins And If It Doesn't Clear Up, Come And See Me Again".

As you might expect of a community with such long associations with the sea, Southsea offers interested visitors the opportunity to seek out many museums replicating how a simple island race used to live in the distant past. Alternatively, if they want to see how a simple island race still does live in the distant past, they can nip on a ferry over to the Isle of Wight.

Southsea is in effect the residential district of Portsmouth and owes its prosperity to Portsmouth's thriving marine industry. This first arose after Henry VIII built a dry dock in the City's port. However, it wasn't really dry in those days. That didn't happen until ownership passed to Southern Water PLC.

Most famously, Portsmouth is associated with Lord Nelson's flagship, the *Victory*, to which visitors flock to see the very spot where the great man fell. It's marked by a brass plaque reading: "At this spot on July 12th 1789, Admiral Horatio Nelson tripped over a bloke screwing a brass plaque to the deck, after inadvertently putting his patch on the wrong eye".

CHICHESTER is often overlooked in favour of its more famous neighbour, Southsea, but as Southsea is a lively, bustling city dripping with a rich history, that comes as no surprise. In the 4th century AD a settlement was founded in Chichester by the Roman XXXIIIVVV Legion, the famous "Fighting Redoubtable Stutterers", who were actually supposed to found Chester. In the late 16th century, Arab dhows plying cargoes of exotic spices along the Red Sea coast down the Horn of Africa and into Zanzibar, sought another entrepôt from which to

trade precious stones with white slave traders and the tribes of the Serengeti. Luckily they discovered Dar Es Salaam, so didn't ever get as far as Chichester.

Chichester grew steadily and today is a market town centred around just four main streets: North Street, South Street, East Street and West Street. Originally there were more, but they were pulled down as too many visiting merchants became hopelessly lost. The city guidebook of 1423 advises that to reach the town centre from the harbour: "… go North up

South Street, turn East along West Street, then South along North-West Street and West into South-East Street before turning North again along South-by-South-West Street then into West-by-South-West Street, taking care to ignore North-East-by-South-West-by-East-North-East-by-West-East Street which is a dead end, and then it's first on your left".

BRIGHTON is the elegant seaside town immortalised unmistakably in Graham Greene's novel *Our Man in Havana*. It was also the motivation for works such as *Vanity Fair* and

Dombey and Son, and was, most famously, the inspiration for Stan Getz's classic bossa nova hit "The Girl From Ipanema". According to legend, during a visit in the early sixties, Mr Getz was driving along the sea front when he noticed an attractively dressed young woman whose every movement turned men's heads, so he stopped at the kerbside to ask if she could sing. The magistrates didn't believe him either, so he was fined ten guineas and deported back to Brazil. And that's why we never got to hear his other great song: "The Girl Called Easy Lil from Burgess Hill".

Brighton was no more than a poor fishing village until the middle 18th century, when the therapeutic benefits of sea bathing were discovered by a general practitioner, Dr Richard Russell. Dr Russell's 25,000 word prescription for a healthy bathing regime would have been the definitive text on the subject, had anyone been able to read it.

In 1782, the Prince Regent came to Brighton with his Court and laid the foundations of the newly fashionable town, having taken a bricklaying evening course to keep himself occupied while waiting for his father to die. He commissioned Nash and Holland to build the fairy tale-like Royal Pavilion, where the young prince courted his many lovers and is even rumoured to have illicitly married. If only the walls of its many chambers could speak, what fascinating stories they might tell us about the history of internal load-bearing structures.

Kiss of Death

Where does one look to find eternal love? The English ladies tennis team scoreboard would be an obvious start. But for many single men it can be hard enough just asking someone out for the evening. Assuming they do manage it, here are some of the panellists' suggestions of remarks they might well consider avoiding on a first date ...

- "Hello. That's the foreplay over."
- **"So, when's it due?"**
- "Well, that was a lovely evening, and with service included it'll cost you two hundred and fifty guineas."
- **"I've just noticed – your eyes match the spinach in your teeth."**
- "Your place or back to the sheltered accommodation?"
- **"Let's go for a run in the Skoda."**
- "Oh, what a lovely dress. I can't wait to try it on."
- **"What's your sister's phone number?"**
- "Oh, are those flowers for me?"

- **"My God, if you're half the woman your mother was ..."**
- "Your hair looks so natural, particularly the left nostril."
- **"I expect this is a whole new experience for you – trainspotting."**
- "Yes, I won first prize in a Robert Maxwell look-a-like competition. Of course I wouldn't have stood a chance if you'd entered."
- **"Don't worry love, the silent ones are the worst, aren't they?"**
- "May I whisper in your ear? That way you may not notice the halitosis."

Topical Nursery Rhymes

Though often taken for granted, the nursery rhyme is part of an age-old oral tradition. Such rhymes should certainly not be dismissed as mere nonsense, since many of them refer to genuine historical characters and incidents. Humpty Dumpty, interestingly enough, was in fact the unfortunate Sir Humpty Fitzdumpty, a very large Elizabethan egg, who fell off a wall. For parents who are concerned that the traditional nursery rhyme contains little of relevance for the 21st Century toddler, here are some updated versions they may find preferable ...

This little piggy went to market,
This little piggy stayed at home,
This little piggy had roast beef
And now he thinks he's a duck.

Mary had a little lamb,
Its fleece was white as snow,
A Frenchman put a match to it
And now it's all aglow.

Ride a cock horse to Banbury Cross
To see a fine lady upon a white horse;
With rings on her navel and studs on her lip,
Who'd have thought nipple rings would ever be hip?

Old King Cole was a merry old soul
And a merry old soul was he,
He called for his pipe
And he called for his bowl
And had a colonic irrigation.

Georgie Porgie, pudding and pie
Went into the gents – now we all know why.

There was an old woman who lived in a shoe,
She had so many children
She didn't know what to do ...
Obviously.

Simple Simon wore a walkman going to the fair.
Said Simple Simon to the pieman: "What?"

Little Boy Blue,
Come blow your horn,
You must be very supple.

Little Miss Muffet sat on a tuffet,
Eating her curds and whey.
There came a big spider,
Who sat down beside her ...
At least he said he was a spider.

Old Mother Hubbard

Old Mother Hubbard
Went to the cupboard
To get her poor dog a bone
But when she got there
The cupboard was bare
Because she'd bought too many
lottery tickets.

Hickory Dickory Dock,
The mouse ran up the clock,
The clock struck
And the mouse came out in sympathy.

There was a crooked man and he walked a crooked mile,
He found a crooked sixpence against a crooked stile,
He bought a crooked cat which caught a crooked mouse
And they all lived together till he fell off his yacht.

Wee Willie Winkie runs through the town,
Upstairs and downstairs in his nightgown.
In an out of houses and along seaside piers
And when they finally catch him, he'll get ten years.

Hey diddle-diddle, the cat and the fiddle,
The cow jumped over the moon.
The little dog laughed to see such sport
And scored some more stuff on a spoon.

The grand old Duke of York,
He had ten thousand men,
But then again, you know how people talk.

Jack Sprat would eat no fat,
His wife would eat no lean
And so between them both, you see
They had very little in common.

Ladybird, ladybird,
Fly away home,
Your house is on fire
And your children have been put in
contact with the local social
services.

Invitation Cards

You'd be surprised just how many people enjoy poring over the society pages of magazines like *Harpers* or *Vogue*, and who like nothing better than spending half an hour with their nose stuck in this week's *Lady*. However, if you're organising a society do yourself, it has become "de rigueur" to ensure that the right celebrity guest is in attendance. For example, if you're thinking of putting on a seven-course banquet, you might want to request the presence of the Duchess of York, who has been known to drop everything for a good bash on a groaning table. You'll also need the right invitation cards ...

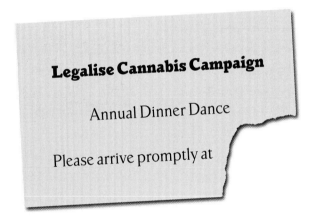

Legalise Cannabis Campaign

Annual Dinner Dance

Please arrive promptly at

The Committee of the Agoraphobics' Society
will be
At Home

The Guild of Greengrocers
Annual Ball
Dinner at 7.30
Cabbages at 12 o'clock

The Society of Knee Surgeons
Cartilages at 11

William Hague
requests the pleasure of your company
at a f-f-f-yon wine tasting
Drinks at f-f-f-f-five

You are invited to
The Dyslexic's Ball
Please RPVSAP

The Haemorrhoid Sufferers' Dinner
(Actually, it's a stand-up buffet)
Toast: Absent enemas

The Tellytubbies' Ball

Drinkie-winkies 7

La-last orders 11

Po's adjacent

Speaker: Dipsy

The Cannibal Society

invites you to a

Finger Buffet

8 for 8.30

(If you're late, we'll keep an eye out for you.)

You're invited to

The Today Programme Ball

RSVP

Are you coming? It's a fairly simple question

England Test Team Ball

Starts at 11

All out by 12

The Lada Drivers' Club

7.30 for 11

Michael Jackson's Birthday Party

7–8

Older children by arrangement

Friends of Michael Winner Evening

Could the two of you arrive about 7?

You are invited to

The Psychics' Ball

You know where

You know when

We know you're coming

Fighter Squadron Reunion

7.30 for 8

Bandits at 12 o'clock

Bookies' Union Big Day Out

At The Gold Cup Steakhouse

Afternoon Tea 5–4

Disco Dancing 11–1 favourite

Misquotations

It's surprising how many of us misquote famous quotations. One line that is frequently muddled is that famous retort of Oscar Wilde: "I have nothing to declare but a bottle of vodka and 200 cigarettes". Or there are those fateful words of Neville Chamberlain: "I have in my hands a piece of paper; would somebody pass a new roll under the door, please?" Here are some others that are often confused ...

- **Play it Sam, play ...**
  the last movement of Shostakovich's 5th piano concerto in E minor and make it snappy.
- **The best laid plans of mice and men ...**
  seldom coincide.
- **Of all the gin joints in all the towns in all the world, she walks into ...**
  a lamppost.
- **We shall fight on the beaches, we shall fight on the landing grounds, we shall fight in the fields and in the streets, we shall fight in the hills, we shall never ...**
  go near the Germans.
- **Should auld acquaintance be forgot and never brought to mind?**
  Yes.
- **Oh, give me a home where the buffalo ...**
  don't lie around on the sofa eating crisps.
- **Walls have ears ...**
  but Lyon's Maid has stripey bits.

- **The King asked the Queen and the Queen asked the dairy maid, could we have some ...**
  three-in-a-bed sex romps.
- **Genius is 2% inspiration and ...**
  99% arithmetic.
- **15 men on a dead man's chest ...**
  I always thought rugby football was dangerous.
- **Frankly, my dear I don't give a ...**
  discount.
- **'Twas brillig and the slithy toves did gyre and gimble in the wabe ...**
  John Cole, BBC News, Westminster.
- **If you can keep your head when all about you are losing theirs ...**
  You'll be taller than anybody else.
- **I met a traveller from an antique land, who said ...**
  has Humph still got a band?
- **If God did not exist, it would be necessary to ...**
  break it very gently to the Pope.

- **Mad dogs and Englishmen go ...**
  Woof, woof! Bring back Maggie!
- **My love is like a red, red ...**
  well, see for yourself, doctor.
- **One small step for man ...**
  a taxi ride for Ronnie Corbett.
- **If Wales could be rolled out flat as England, it would ...**
  be known as the Hereford bypass.
- **Some chicken, some neck ...**
  some peas and some roast potatoes.
- **The curfew tolls the knell of parting day,**
  The lowing herd winds slowly o'er the lea,
  The ploughman homeward plods his weary way ...
  Thomas Grey, News At Ten, Country Churchyard.

QUOTING SHAKESPEARE

- **Alas poor Yorrick, I knew ...**
  he wasn't well at breakfast.
- **Et tu ...**
  but couldn't manage three Shredded Wheat.
- **Shall I compare thee to a summer's day? Thou art more ...**
  wet and windy, with a cold front moving in from the South.
- **To be or not to be ...**
  that is the apiarist's dilemma.

- **It is a wise father that knows his own ...**
  blood group.
- **When shall we three meet again? In thunder, lightning or in ...**
  Sainburys.
- **It was a lover and his lass, with a ...**
  large egg whisk.
- **The quality of mercy is not strained ...**
  but I can recommend the cabbage.
- **Blow wind and crack your cheeks ...**
  but for God's sake, put the cat out first.

Historical Headlines

In days of yore, long before the daily papers enjoyed computer-based news gathering, messages of great importance were relayed across the distant reaches of the Kingdom along a series of huge beacons lit by hilltop villages. Of course, by far the most common message was: "Help! Our hilltop village is on fire!" Here are the teams' suggestions of how today's newspapers and periodicals might have reported certain historical events.

WILLIAM CAXTON INVENTS PRINTING PRESS

- The Guardian: Newt Technolody Spills End To Mispronts
- **The Daily Mail: Protect Our Children From The Menace Of The Printed Word**
- The Daily Express: Monks Down Quills In Protest
- **The Mirror: Up Yours, Gutenberg!**
- The Sun: Monks Still Necessary To Illuminate Page Three Wench
- **Publisher's Weekly: Fly Fishing By J R Hartley Made Possible By Good Old Middle Ages**
- Tailor & Cutter: Caxton Says It Also Does Trousers
- **The Guardian: Caxton Shows Off New Dress**
- The Spectator: Book Of The Decade Club To Go Monthly

THE DEATH OF SAMSON

- The Times: Samson Obituary – Two Columns – Page 8
- **The Daily Express: Ban Scissors Campaign Grows**
- New Musical Express: Oh, Oh, Oh, Delilah!
- **The Stage: Fears For Bruce Forsyth's Strength**
- The Daily Telegraph: Police Chief Says He Was An Accident Waiting To Happen
- **The Guardian – Corrections & Clarifications page: Delilah's statement should have read "I love cutting men's locks off"**

JULIUS CAESAR INVADES BRITAIN

- **The Colchester Evening Gazette: Tesco Sells Out Of Pizzas**
- The Sun: Veni Vidi Gotcha!
- **The Financial Times: FT Index Up 423 Points On Expectation Of Huge Road Building Scheme**
- British Medical Journal: Roman Army Doctors Set Up Veni Vici Vidi Clinic
- **Melody Maker: Veni, Vidi, Vici, Mick And Titch Go To Number One**
- The Daily Express: Romans Invade – No Britons Involved

JOAN OF ARC BURNS AT STAKE

- Green News: Wood Burning French – Threat To Ozone Layer
- **The Star: Phew, What A Scorcher!**
- The Daily Mail: "English Hooligans Burnt My Daughter" Says Mrs Arc
- **Le Figaro: Government Spokesman Says Smoking Can Seriously Damage Your Health**
- The Cricketer: England Wins Ashes
- **The Sun: French Filly Flambé**

Film Club

WELSH

Played while Samantha was off on a mountaineering course with a couple of chaps. She said to take part they had to be equipped, like Wales and enjoy a rarebit ...

- Cool Hand Look-You
- **Leek Marvin in Paint Your Dragon**
- Dai Hard
- **Dai Hard II**
- An American In Powys
- **Bring Me The Holyhead Of Alfredo Garcia**
- The Llanfairpwllgwyngyllgoge-rychwyrndrobwyll-llantysiliogo-gogo Between
- **The Good, The Bard and Llanelly**
- Breakfast At Taffy Knees
- **Mad Max Boyce**
- The Eagle Has Llandudno
- **Where Eagles Aberdare**
- Tom Courtenay and Albert Finney in The Welsh Dresser
- **Look-you Bach In Bangor**
- Huw Dares Gwynneth
- **Nine and a Half Leeks**
- Evans Can Wait
- **Shake, Rattle and Rhyll**
- Eissteddfod Zebra
- **A Fishguard Called Rhonda**
- The tragic-comic romance Sheepless In Seattle
- **... and its heart-warming sequel When Harry Met Dolly**
- The Sheep That Died Of Shame
- **Yach-y-Daadle Dandy**
- Bob And Carol And Dill And Thomas
- **And Haverfordwest Was Won**

SMOKERS

Played while Samantha nipped backstage to enjoy 20 king-size Players.

- Whose Afraid Of Virginia Slims
- **Part of the Tar Wars Trilogy – The**
- **Empire Strikes A Light**
- Nicotine And Alexandra
- **Reservoir Dog Ends**
- Full Menthol Packet
- **The Lung Goodbye starring Chesty Conklin and Stubby Kaye**
- El Cig
- **Cheroots Of Fire**
- Hamlet
- **The Grapes of Rothmans**
- Gasper The Friendly Ghost
- **Smokey And They've Banned It**
- Look Baccy In Anger
- **Jurassic Park Drive – See The Bronchitis Walk!**
- Follow That Camel
- **Nicoteenage Mutant Ninja Turtles II**
- I Was A Fugitive From A Chain Smoker
- **Look Who's Toking**
- Any snuff movie
- **Bring Me The Benson & Hedges Of Alfredo Garcia.**

LAUNDERETTE ATTENDANTS

Played while Samantha and Humph nipped out for a quick tumble (great value at only 20p) and later to drop into Sketchleys to put some starch into his little dickie.

- No Socks Please, We're British
- **Dry Hard**
- Back To The New Ariel Future
- **The Spy Who Came In For The Bold**
- Cool Wash Luke
- **You Only Rinse Twice**
- Non Bio East Of Java
- **The Smalls Of Monte Zuma starring Laundry Hepburn and Ariel Flynn**
- Some Like It Hot Wash
- **On The Bleach**
- Sink The Skidmark
- **Bring Me The Vest Of Alfredo Garcia.**

Humph's Gazetteer of the British Isles

LIVERPOOL has a linguistic derivation of some considerable historical interest. Guidebooks relate that the city took its name from two Old English words meaning "Boggy Water", and the name is first mentioned in the Anglo Saxon Chronicle when King Edmund sailed up a creek of the Mersey and discovered "Muddy Pools", who went on to become one of the greatest blues guitarists of the 9th century.

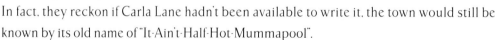

However, some historians believe there is a more plausible explanation for the name "Liverpool", suggesting that it may actually have come from the famous *Liver Birds*. In fact, they reckon if Carla Lane hadn't been available to write it, the town would still be known by its old name of "It-Ain't-Half-Hot-Mummapool".

Famous Liverpudlians ("Scousers"), include Jimmy Tarbuck ("Tarby"), Cilla Black ("Cilla") and Les Dennis ("that bloke off the telly"). Cilla and Tarby, true to their proud roots in Everton and Toxteth, still live very close by in Marbella.

HARROGATE boasts a fine literary pedigree. In the beautifully constructed, finely honed and well researched novels of James Herriot, for example, it appears as "Brawton", while in the works of Lord Archer it features as "Pnom Penh".

The town's popularity grew after one William Slingsby discovered a local spa, and down four centuries, visitors have been amazed by the health-giving properties of the water here. Today, of course, they are amazed to find that Harrogate's spa is the only source of water of any description in Yorkshire.

BUXTON is another delightful spa town but it has few claims to fame other than the fact that it was the birthplace of actor and comedian Tim Brooke-Taylor. In honour of his many achievements, Buxton recently bestowed upon Tim the freedom of the city of Sheffield.

Buxton is probably best known for its radioactive springs, but these were all destroyed after every Austin Allegro to which they had been fitted was recalled by the main dealers and replaced under warranty.

Like other places in the Peak District, Buxton still practises the ancient ritual of "well-dressing". This involves setting up a wooden sacred image covered with clay and then coating it with a mosaic of flower petals, leaves, moss and grass cuttings. The whole process can last up to three weeks and everyone is welcome. Anyone thinking they might enjoy a visit to Buxton to witness this really ought to get a life.

CHESTER is the historic Cheshire city whose good people once returned Gy les Brandreth as an MP. And who can blame them?

The name "Chester" derives from the Latin "Castra Devana", meaning a riverside garrison. It was named by the infamous Roman Commander "Julius Clarius", who was sent ahead of the approaching army to find a suitable location for Caesar's XXth Legion. Clarius terrified the local population when he marched into the town and proclaimed: "I am on the look out for Caesar's Camp". After overindulging in the many houses of ill-repute, he became ill and spent some months being treated at the 495 clinic. Parts of a stone tablet in the city museum recount the event: "CLARIVS CLAPPVS SIC" and go on to describe his wife as "LIVID", which was quite an advanced age for those days.

Chester has uniquely preserved its ancient city walls. Leading up to them on the north side are the "Wishing Steps". Local custom says that anyone who can run up and down these 127 steps twice without drawing breath will have his wish fulfilled. This has proved to be true for several hopefuls whose wish was apparently to turn blue and collapse with oxygen starvation brought on by self-induced asphyxia.

LEEDS still has many reminders of the part this fine Yorkshire town played in the Industrial Revolution. Starting at nearby Middleton is the oldest surviving railway in England. With its original line and stock virtually unchanged since 1758, it was recently privatised and renamed the Midland Main Line to Euston.

Founded on textiles, until 1969 Leeds had the world's largest surviving woollen mill. Then someone pulled at a loose thread and the whole building unravelled.

No visit to Leeds would be complete without taking in the city's art gallery. Its collection includes work from L S Lowrie's "Matchstick Men" period, followed by his "Pipe-cleaner People" period and finally his "Other Unrealistic Body Shapes Fashioned from Smokers General Requisites" period. Sadly, Rosetti's Pre-Raphaelite portrait of the young Queen Victoria as the Goddess Aphrodite drinking from the fountain of Zeus is no longer on display. This was found to be a fake after cleaning revealed she was wearing a Leeds Rugby League Club Jersey – a silly mistake, as Queen Victoria was a well-known Hull Kingston Rovers supporter.

Several world-famous comic writers were born in Leeds. Everybody in the city has heard of Alan Bennett and Barry Cryer has heard of him as well. Amongst its many show-biz connections, Leeds is probably best known to TV viewers in other parts of the country for its City Varieties Theatre, home of *The Good Old Days* and its MC, Leonard Sachs; exceptionally, elegantly, eloquently, eruditely fond reminders of the years before BBC entertainment shows became inevitably, irretrievably, irredeemably, inconsequential inanities.

Name Dropping

A marvellous game which you too can now play in the comfort of your own home. You can score yourself according to the weight of name correctly identified, on a scale up to ten for a Greta Garbo, a Frank Sinatra or a Humphrey Lyttelton, down to one for a Wincey Willis or a Bob Holness. The "Richard Whiteley" name score is in the second place of decimals, while a "Nicholas Parsons" will get you disqualified and drug tested. Good luck!

Hello Tim. You won't guess who we cooked supper for last night.

You've got a cook, haven't you?

No, we had to sue Cook for stealing.

Well, there's nothing worse than a robbin' cook.

The kids cooked it on the new Aga. You know there's so much the oven can't do that the Aga can. I'm absolutely adamant about it.

Did you give the kids orders like: "John, peel the potatoes; Stephen, fry the onions; Patrick, more salt, please; James, boil the pig's head"?

That last one was just a description. Haven't your Jeremy and Sean been working in Sketchleys?

Yes, Sean operates the tumble-drier and Jeremy irons.

I must say, you and Victoria certainly have a large family. Do you plan to roger more?

I don't, but Victoria would. According to our bank manager, Michael, we can't really afford it. But I told Michael flatly, I said "Cough up". You bank with Lloyds, don't you?

No, but Tony banks there. He says they'll sting you just for saying "Good morning".

Have you seen this? I've found something very interesting in this *Innovations* catalogue.

That's a novelty. What is it?

It's something to help the kids keep their *Toytown* characters tidy.

Is it called a "Noddy holder"?

Goodness no! What a ridiculous name.

Ten things you never knew about

Colin Sell

(And ten things you probably did)

1. Colin Sell was born into a family of virtuoso musicians; his soprano mother sang with Caruso and Melba, and his father, in between co-writing with Britten and Coward, helped Glenn Miller arrive at his unique big band brass sound. Colin attended the Vienna Conservatoire from the age of 3, where he was Best In Year on the harpsichord, viola, ondes Martenot, crumhorn and oboe. He has since written countless Hollywood movie scores for Hitchcock, Kubrick and Altman, was for some years musical director at the New York Metropolitan Opera House, and has produced albums for the Beatles, the Rolling Stones, Madonna and Elvis Costello. But the Colin Sell we're talking about here is the one who bangs the piano on *I'm Sorry I Haven't A Clue*.

2. In the *Farmers' Weekly*'s review of Colin's first professional performance at a Young Farmers' Set-a-Side and Subsidy charity hop near Cirencester, it stated: "Colin Sell's playing was much enhanced when he had a go at singing as well". It should have read "Colin Sell's playing was much enhanced when he had a goat singing as well".

3. Colin's musical influences are known to be Middle Eastern in origin. Mostly Shiite.

4. Colin was once asked to give a talk at the Richard Wagner Society after they'd heard he had mastered the full complexity of the Ring Cycle. However, after sitting through a three-hour dissertation on his new twin-tub washing machine, they realised he had actually figured out how to get the rinse cycle to work.

5. Last year Colin was invited to play at a special U2 gig. What fine reunion dances those German submarine crews enjoy.

6. When Colin worked with pop sensation Bjork, he made frequent trips to Iceland, or if they were shut, she used to send him to Bejam.

7. During a recent performance, Colin had piles of underwear thrown at him. As a result of the disturbance, Wash-O-Matic Limited have banned him for life from busking in all their launderettes.

8. **Back in the 1970s, Colin once produced 10cc. But the doctor needed a bigger sample and asked him to try again with the tap running.**

9. For three years running, Colin has won the award for "Best Use of Harmony". The Royal Society of Hairdressers say he cleverly uses it to keep the fringe out of his eyes, giving total control without ever becoming too greasy.

10. **There is now a website for Colin's many fans. Everyone who shares his passion for vintage kitchen extractor equipment can find it at www.co//in@se//vent.axia**

11. Colin has recently decided he'd like to branch into artist management and has a dream of handling the Spice Girls. Mrs Sell says it's the only thing that gets him up in the morning.

12. **Whenever top professional musicians hear the name "Colin Sell", they are always keen for news of the "Old Maestro". At the moment it's being welded up after failing its MOT again, so Colin's back to using his scooter.**

13. It has recently been discovered that Colin has perfect pitch. So, if your garage roof needs re-felting, why not give him a call?

14. **Colin has recently been entertaining shipping on a nonstop tour of sea areas and inshore waters, and was reviewed briefly in the influential** Shipping Forecast Gazette: **It read: "Mainly variable, becoming poor".**

15. Colin's piano playing is believed by faith healers to hold miraculous powers. It once made a blind man deaf.

16. **Colin completes a new album every year. What a fine service he says he gets from Supersnaps.**

17. Colin's first TV appearance was when he played the mouth organ in Black Lace. Opportunity Knocks said it was the worst novelty drag act they'd ever had on the show.

18. **Colin's name first came to public notice when he was asked to fire a cannon at the end of the 1812. The Investigation Report by British Transport Police said that if his aim had been better he would have destroyed the entire buffet car.**

19. In 1986, Bob Geldof asked Colin to go to Wembley for Band Aid. But when he got there he found the chemists was shut so he had to buy them at Boots in Dollis Hill instead.

20. **There's many a pianist who would give their right arm to play like Colin Sell. In fact, losing an arm would be a very good way to perfect the technique.**

Celebrity Misquotes

And now the results of a game which grew out of the old Somerset saying: "Of all the gin joints in all the towns in all the world, you had to walk into Minehead". While there are plentiful records documenting things that famous people have said, there are precious few records of things they never said. In fact, if it wasn't for our daily newspapers, we'd have precious little idea who hadn't said what at all.

- **"It's engaged!"**
  Alexander Graham Bell
- "I won't be two seconds.
  I'll just put my make-up on."
  Barbara Cartland
- **"My mother-in-law ..."**
  Julian Clary
- "I thought very carefully before I made the tackle as my prime concern was to win the ball cleanly."
  Vinnie Jones
- **"Should Herr Hitler ever set foot on the shores of our beloved country, you will not see my baggy striped trousers for dust."**
  Winston Churchill
- "I was so drunk last night, I ended up going home with a couple of sailors."
  Mother Teresa
- **"Are you all right for the weekend, sir?"**
  The Pope
- "Open the box!"
  Dracula

- **"One hundred and eighty!"**
  General Custer
- "Bernard Manning, now he does amuse us."
  Queen Victoria
- **"That Margaret Roberts, she looks a bit useful."**
  Ted Heath
- "What do you mean, you're pregnant?"
  Cliff Richard
- **"I'll take the pair."**
  Long John Silver
- "Tunes."
  Melvyn Bragg
- **"I want a Walkman for Christmas."**
  Van Gogh
- "Sorry love, that's a bit over the top."
  Ken Russell
- **"Is there someone else?"**
  Eve (to Adam)
- "Can you hear me at the back?"
  Ian Paisley
- **"Oh, they're free – I'll take ten."**
  Moses

- "I think it could do with a re-write."
  Jeffrey Archer
- **"Sorry, I only do floors."**
  Michaelangelo
- "'Ere mush, you trying to be funny?"
  Gandhi
- **"I'm a bum and tit woman myself."**
  Mary Whitehouse
- "Oh, I wouldn't appear on that!"
  Carol Vorderman
- **"Could you make it a cheque?"**
  Judas Escariot
- "It's the British players that worry me."
  Pete Sampras
- **"My goodness, I'd like to get that**
  Tim Brooke-Taylor under the
  mistletoe."
  Michelle Pffeifer
- "Oh great, I've been looking for those
  gloves."
  O J Simpson
- **"No, no, I'll pay!"**
  The Duchess of York
- "It looks just like it, doesn't it?"
  Pablo Picasso
- **"Total bastards shall inherit**
  the earth."
  Jesus Christ
- "Can't you cavaliers be serious for one
  moment?"
  Frans Hals

- **"Your private life is no concern**
  of mine."
  Jerry Springer
- "There's no need to shout."
  Beethoven
- **"I know my limitations."**
  Anthea Turner
- "Well, I suppose we don't have to go
  this way."
  The Orange Order
- **"A half bottle of Optrex, please."**
  Horatio Nelson
- "Hello!"
  Marcel Marceau
- **"I'm sure there's a perfectly**
  rational scientific explanation
  for it."
  St Paul
- "No, you talk – I'll listen."
  Clive Anderson
- **"But I would like to be friends."**
  Henry VIII
- "Of course, I'm no expert on the subject."
  Jonathan Miller
- **"No need to get nasty."**
  The Marquis de Sade
- "What do we want? A rise! When do we
  want it? Now! Out! Out! Out!"
  Florence Nightingale
- **"Please! I'm married!"**
  Bill Clinton

Sound Charades

The round inspired by the popular TV show *Give Us A Clue*, where Lionel Blair and Una Stubbs memorably got up off the sofa and performed against the clock. In the original version, players weren't allowed to speak – the source of much mirth and hilarity. In our version they were. Here are some more to try at home ...

FILM – ONE WORD

MAN 1: *(Clearly in some discomfort)* Excuse me, I wonder if you could help me?

MAN 2: Ah yes. Turn left at the elephant house, cross over by the penguins, carry on past the lions' cage and it's third on your right.

MAN 1: Thank you very much.

(Zulu)

BOOK, FILM AND PLAY
FOUR WORDS

CUSTOMER: Good morning.

ASSISTANT: Ah, good morning, sir. What can I do for you?

CUSTOMER: I'd like to buy a cricket bat, please.

ASSISTANT: A cricket bat – we have a very large selection, as you can see.

(SOUND EFFECT: FARTING SOUND)

ASSISTANT: Reg! I'm serving a customer in here! Sorry about that, sir, perhaps I can show you some ...

(SOUND EFFECT: FARTING SOUND)

ASSISTANT: Reg! Can't you go outside or something. I do apologise, sir. Here we are – here we have the Compton Classic ...

(SOUND EFFECT: FARTING SOUND)

ASSISTANT: Reg, if you don't stop that I'm going to come up and take that trombone away from you.

(Wind In The Willows)

TWO FILMS - ONE WORD

DOCTOR: Good morning. how's the patient today?

CONSULTANT: Not very well, I'm afraid.

DOCTOR: What!? But He's the Supreme Being, the Creator of the World.

CONSULTANT: That's as may be, but he fell ill yesterday and today he's worse.

(Godzilla)

FILM - TWO WORDS

GUISEPPE: Uno pollo, due pollo, tres pollo, quattro pollo.

ANTONIO: Hey! Guiseppe! How manya times I tella you notta to count your chickens?

GUISEPPE: Oh. Abouta thirteen times.

(Apollo 13)

FILM - THREE WORDS

HAMISH: Hello Dougal. Oh. I see you've got your family with you.

DOUGAL: Oh aye, Hamish, I've brought the bairns. Here's wee Victoria. Say hello to Uncle Hamish. And there's wee Euston.

HAMISH: I think I've met this wee soul Paddington. I think I recognise him.

DOUGAL: King's Cross and Liverpool Street are at home just now.

HAMISH: Oh, I did hear that your good lady was expecting?

DOUGAL: Oh aye, that's true, she's 20 minutes overdue.

(The Railway Children)

FILM - TWO WORDS

VOICE 1: Hey, you know that Colin Sell?

VOICE 2: Yeah?

VOICE 2: What's he playing at?

(The Piano)

Misleading Advice

With its perfect climate, clean beaches and reliable public transport system, Britain holds many attractions for the first-time visitor to these shores. Yet it can also be quite confusing to the tourist unfamiliar with our unique island culture. Here are some helpful pointers ...

- In Scotland, haggis is the Gaelic word for a vegetarian dish.
- **The citizens of Glasgow love to hear foreigners imitating their accent, especially in a pub on a Friday night.**
- Traffic wardens are always addressed as "Tit Face!"
- **If you need to get across London in a hurry, try the Bakerloo line.**
- Men: Try midnight orienteering on Hampstead Heath.
- **Barbara Windsor is a member of the Royal Family.**
- The English for lavatory is "Pizza Hut".
- **Please do not consult your maps in the middle of the pavement - zebra crossings are provided for this purpose.**
- Warning - Pickpockets: Trafalgar Square is now heavily policed - you'd do better in Bond Street.
- **Don't miss Wimbledon Fortnight, but remember to get there early to book the court.**
- Always kiss nightclub bouncers.
- **Put your money on England in the cricket - the Australian fast bowlers are a spent force.**
- Millwall fans are known as fairies.
- **You can time your journey by checking the timetable posted at any bus stop.**
- It's considered bad form to fall asleep in the theatre - so book a few wake-up calls on your mobile phone.
- **Do remember that Yorkshiremen love to have the piss taken out of them.**
- People in a queue are actually waiting for you to go first.
- **Genuine Rolex watches are so in demand, they're sold on the streets before they can reach the shops.**
- American motorists: remember that in Britain you won't be able to fill up your car with "gasoline" - we call it "diesel".
- **A good ice-breaker at dinner parties is how dreadful it must have been for the Germans during the War.**

- Outside Buckingham Palace it is customary to shout: "We want Fergie!"
- **Visitors to the Garrick Club are reminded that it is customary to dress as Spice Girls.**
- Ask for the delicious bacon sandwiches at Bloom's Kosher restaurant.
- **To hear English spoken as it should be, tune in to the Teletubbies.**
- Don't miss The Trooping Of The Colour, where you can join in the traditional game of "Grab The Flag".
- **Join in the raven shooting at the Tower of London.**
- It is quite legal to relieve yourself on the near left leg of a police horse.

- **Pianist Alfred Brendel is appearing tonight at the Royal Albert Hall, and remember – it's karaoke night!**
- If you are staying with a British family, it is considered polite on leaving to pay their council tax.
- **The old market in Bond Street is worth a visit, but don't forget to haggle.**
- See the waxworks in the House of Lords.
- **If you see any red and white cones on the motorway – pick them up.**
- Don't forget to pack your shotguns because there's fine hunting at Longleat, Whipsnade and Windsor Safari Park.

- **When entering the Gents, it is protocol to smile at everyone and shout out: "Hello, naughty!"**
- Ladies, when in an Anglican church, please join in the sermon.
- **If travelling by rail, rest assured that your train will be on time and the inspector will be pleased to give you any information you may require.**
- Cheerful porters at any railway station will carry your luggage.
- **In our older train carriages you'll find comfortable hammocks located above the seats.**
- Go into any public house and shout: "Mine's a large Fatima Whitbread!"
- **Make use of the telephones in our one-person public lavatories.**
- Do take advantage of London's self-drive taxis. They're easily identified by the flashing blue light on the top.
- **Lonely Hearts: Try writing your phone number in heavy magic marker on the inside of phone booths.**
- Prostitution is now legal in Britain and anyone can get themselves fixed up simply by ringing the organiser, Mrs Mary Whitehouse.

- **Feeling peckish? On most streets you will find complimentary cats and dogs.**
- You always know where you are with Radio 4.
- **Go to an O'Neill's bar for an authentic taste of old Ireland.**
- Before leaving a swimming pool it is considered polite to top it up.
- **Our prostitutes stand outside offices smoking cigarettes.**
- Taxi driving is a lonely life – encourage drivers to share their opinions.

Postbag

ON THE SUBJECT OF CHANGES TO THE RADIO 4 SCHEDULE:

Dear Shula,

How awful they should have moved the "Moral Maze" from its traditional time to be hidden away in some obscure slot. You can imagine my horror and dismay when I tuned in specially and found I hadn't missed it yet!

Yours faithfully,

Mrs Trellis,

North Wales

PS What about pronunciation? One day it's a new "skedule"; the next it's a new "shedule". Either way Radio 4, stop shunting the skedule about!

ON THE SUBJECT OF THE 22ND SERIES OF *I'M SORRY I HAVEN'T A CLUE*:

Dear Trevor Brooking-Taylor,

Congratulations! Congratulations! Congratulations!

These are my three favourite Cliff Richard records.

Yours faithfully,

Mrs Trellis,

North Wales

ON THE SUBJECT OF YOUNG COUPLES SETTING UP HOME TOGETHER:

Dear Bamber,

It's never good policy to store tubes of Superglue and Vaseline in the same cupboard. If a young wife is in a hurry, it's all too easy to get them muddled up. I did once and you can guess what happened. The broken spout fell off my teapot.

Yours faithfully,

Mrs Trellis,

North Wales

ON THE SUBJECT OF BAD LANGUAGE ON BBC RADIO:

Dear Kenton,

I was appalled on tuning in this morning to be bombarded with a torrent of blatant filth. With terms such as "large firm", "holding up well", "satisfying performance" and worst of all "job blows", it was the most offensive edition of the *Today Programme Business Report* ever.

Yours disgustedly,

Mrs Trellis,

Wild Shag Cottage,

Upper Sheepsbottom Lane,

Much Humping on Sea

Humph's Gazetteer
of the British Isles

ISLINGTON A settlement was first mentioned here in Anglo-Saxon times as "Gislandune", or "Hill of Gisla". No one now knows who Gisla was and in modern times the name is only ever used by the drug-crazed sadist who sets the *Guardian* Cryptic Crossword. The hill is recorded as being close to the site where Bodicea (originally pronounced "Boodikka" before later being pronounced dead) fought the Romans at Islington Spa, before taking on the Iceni at Camden Sainsburys.

Fleeing from London in 1372, Edward II was captured close by, in what was then Middlesex Forest. The hapless monarch later suffered a painful death at the hands of a torturer wielding a red hot poker after uttering those famous last words: "You know where you can stick that for a kick-off".

Later still, Sir Walter Raleigh settled briefly in Islington. The man who had successfully introduced the nation to potatoes and tobacco set about opening his famous bicycle factory in Upper Street. It soon became fashionable at court to be seen riding either the Raleigh Tourer or the Raleigh BMX and it is widely rumoured that Queen Elizabeth I herself enjoyed some exhilarating rides on the sturdy Raleigh Chopper.

Today, Islington is the haunt of artists and writers, a trend started by Daniel Defoe. Working on early drafts of *Robinson Crusoe*, he found himself wanting for a character name. Glancing round his study, Defoe's eye fell upon the calendar and a particular day inspired him to name Crusoe's native sidekick: "Man Pancake".

HACKNEY is an ancient community steeped in history. Nestling in the lea of the Sussex Downs, where chalk streams tumble over lush, rolling meadowland, plump cherries ripen on sagging bows, bunches of fat hops dry on high poles and acres of maize, wheat and barley wave their nourishing heads in the summer's breeze, would be an unlikely setting for an inner city borough, which is why Hackney isn't situated there.

The name "Hackney" actually derives from a 14th-century French word meaning a workhorse, hence the expression "Hackney Carriage". Interestingly, the words "Hackney Carriage" have no connection with Hackney, the London Borough, which explains why it is impossible ever to find a taxi there.

Hackney is undoubtedly best known for the Hackney Empire. Lasting from about 750 AD well into the 12th century, it covered much of Northern Europe to the Urals and was the constant rival to the expansionist Visigoths, who feared the frequent raids into their territory made by fierce marauding warriors clad in sequined suits and large floppy hats, who terrified the indigenous population with plates of jellied eels. While the Hackney Empire is gone, the habit of frightening foreigners with jellied eels and funny hats remains.

The other reminder of this glorious past is of course the theatre named in memory of the Hackney Empire: the London Palladium. Down the years, this house of variety saw performances from music hall greats such as Charlie Chaplin, W C Fields, Marie Lloyd and Mary Pickford. After one memorable evening when all four appeared on the bill together, Chaplin and W C Fields decided to form a business partnership and United Artists was born. Miffed at having been left out, Marie Lloyd started a high street bank to provide finance for Mary Pickford to launch her world-famous removals firm.

WIMBLEDON is located in the very heart of glitzy London's outskirts. The original village first became known in Tudor times, when, in 1587, the Earl of Exeter established the Royal College of Tennis here in an attempt to fulfil Queen Elizabeth I's wish to see an English player compete in a singles final. It is obviously far too soon to say whether his efforts will be rewarded. The Earl himself, however, did go on to achieve his ambition of entering Queens. He was invariably unseeded.

In Regency times, the village became a fashionable haunt for the likes of Lady Hamilton, who scandalised polite society with her many suitors. This held dire consequences for Lord Nelson when he wagered drunkenly at the gaming table: "If Lady Hamilton isn't completely faithful to me, and me alone, you can pull my left arm off and poke me in the eye with it."

In Victorian times, both Liberty's and William Morris produced fabrics here, while Lord Cardigan fought a duel on the common to promote his range of popular knitwear. Subsequently, he went on to manufacture the cosy woollen headgear developed during the Crimean War, which he named in memory of the Battle of Bobble Hat.

RICHMOND is one of London's most outlying boroughs, situated as it is in North Yorkshire. This interesting community was described in 1945 by the British Council Guide as "the most typically British town". Bearing in mind that in 1945 most British towns had typically been reduced to rubble, this is some compliment indeed. Richmond today is a thriving, bustling place, mainly concerned as it is with the thriving bustle manufacturing industry.

Just across the river from the town proper is the site now famous as the place where Henry VIII had his magnificent Hampton Court. Henry took the palace from Wolsey to provide a home for his new wife, Anne Boleyn. However, she was never comfortable there, complaining that the ceilings were too low. Structural alterations were found to be impossible, as the building was Grade II listed by the English Council for the Preservation of Modern Buildings, and so the King took the only alternative, which was to have Queen Anne shortened by a foot or so.

Superstitions

We all suffer from those peculiar little irrational fears that have come to be known as "superstitions". Tim, for example, believes that it is very bad luck to buy a round of drinks in a pub. Now you can test yourself on some superstitious general knowledge. Here's how the teams got on ...

Q. Complete the following superstitious rhyme:
"A mole on your arm
Can bring you no harm
A mole on your back ..."
A. Wants a lift to the lawn.
(*Ans. Brings money by the sack.*)

Q. Complete the following superstitious saying:
"If the cat in your house is black ..."
A. Phone the fire brigade – only it may be too late.
(*Ans. Of lovers you will have no lack.*)

Q. Complete the following superstitious rhyme:
"A spider in the morning is a sign of sorrow
A spider in the afternoon ..."
A. Is a sign of poor positional play leaving the cue ball hampered by the pink.
(*Ans. Brings worry for tomorrow.*)

Q. What's supposed to happen if you wear rosemary around your neck?
A. You'll have to marry her.
(*Ans. You'll have a better memory.*)

Q. What does it mean if a shrew passes over your foot in Shaftesbury?
A. You'll get shafted in Shrewsbury.
(*Ans. You'll walk with a limp for the rest of your life.*)

Q. Complete the following superstitious rhyme:
"If the wind blows on you through a hole ..."
A. Move to another cubicle.
(*Ans. Say your prayers and mind your soul.*)

Q. Complete the following rhyme recited by Devon girls in front of a bowl of water with the letters of the alphabet in it:
"I place my shoes in the letter "T"
In the hope ..."
A. I'll pass English GCSE.
(*Ans. My true love I shall see.*)

Q. Why is it good luck to throw salt over your left shoulder?
A. It gets the mole off your back.
(*Ans. Salt was seen as a protective substance and evil spirits were supposed to live on your left side.*)

Hitler's Diaries

This next section was inspired by that unfortunate incident when Rupert Murdoch wanted to publish the writings of a notorious dictator in *The Sunday Times*. He did, and we never heard the last of her.
It should not be confused with the old parlour game originally known as "Hitler's Dairy", in which players tried to increase their sales of Gold Top by annexing the Sudetenland ...

WILLIAM WORDSWORTH

Tuesday I awoke this morning. I could hear Dorothy downstairs fossicking about for her dentures in the microwave – she does hate cold teeth of a morning. I opened a window and – bloody daffodils! Miles and miles of the little bastards. A sea of bloody daffodils! A custard lake of daffodils! I hate daffodils! I'm going to suggest to Dorothy that we move.
Thursday Looked at a property in Wandsworth. Stood on Westminster Bridge – bloody awful view! How can people live like this? At least there weren't any bloody daffodils. I like caravan parks. Earth has not anything to show more fair than a decent caravan park.

MACBETH – THANE OF CAWDOR

Monday Had a chat with the sisters. They're planning a new TV cooking series "Have Eye Of Newts For You".
Wednesday 14th New glasses arrived and are excellent. I was right: it is a dagger.
Thursday 4th A group of actors have begged me to change my name to Lord Scottish Play.
Wednesday 9th Everyone's talking about Banquo's goat. Perhaps the glasses are not as good as I thought. I can't see any goat. My hearing aid is working well, though. Must remember to leave a note for the milkman for tomorrow and tomorrow and tomorrow.
Friday 21st Not feeling well. I think I'm d–

THE MAN IN THE IRON MASK

Tuesday 4th Oct. Clean socks. That itch under my nose is back. As I'm not allowed any sharp implements, such as a knitting needle, I have to try to scratch it by pushing a carrot through one of the eyeholes.

Wednesday 5th Oct. Carrot broke off. Now I've got a lump of carrot in here with me. Still, it could be worse. The bloke in the next cell is The Man In The Iron Underpants.

Thursday 6th Oct. Wonder how Crystal Palace are doing?

JOSEPH

Monday Mary gone shopping. Why Christmas always comes when the fields are crowded, I'll never know. Said this to Mary later when she was listening to her Carpenters album. Sent donkey in for service. If it's not back in time, we can hire one.

I said to her: "There's a screw under the saddle ..." Not a titter.

Wednesday Set off. Roads crowded. Tailbacks. A319 to Nazareth exit.

Stopped off at Happy Easter for a snack.

Thursday Arrived at hotel. Wouldn't you know it – they're full. He said the stable annex is free, but we've got to provide our own swaddling clothes. Three wise men arrived. Isn't it typical? You wait ages for a wise man and then three come along at the same time.

MARGARET THATCHER – THE POST DOWNING STREET YEARS

Wednesday 14th April Geoffrey Howe rang for a chat. We agreed to do another karaoke evening. This time I'm going to be Cher.

Tuesday 19th April Awake all night worrying about the Belgrano. John Major rang for advice.

I said: "Jack, the day you need advice is the day I stop break dancing."

Friday I've asked the servants to burn Denis' and my body after the suicide. I can't bear the idea of being strung up on a lamppost like Mussolini. Or was it George Formby?

Proverbs In Translation

Great Britain has bestowed much upon the rest of the world, from exploitative imperialism and BSE to the Duchess of York. And then there is, of course, the English language. One aspect of our versatile tongue that's yet to make an international impact is the proverb. As you will see, many of our traditional sayings can be usefully adapted to suit foreign countries ...

- Africa – Pride comes before a bad moment for a gazelle.
- **Australia – Love is blind, so brace yourself, Sheila.**
- Balkans – See a pin and pick it up, all day long you'll be wondering where the grenade is.
- **Belgium – In for a penny, in for a .66 of a Euro.**
- China – Love me, eat my dog.
- **Eastern Europe – You can't bloody get out of Estonia.**
- France – One man's meat is another man's poisson.

  France – Don't put Descartes before the horse.

  France – Better late than Belgian.

  France – Don't teach your grandmother to suck existentialists.

  France – Red sky at night, shepherd's delight, red sky in the morning. British sheep are on fire.
- **Germany – Achtungs speak louder than words.**

Germany – Laughter is the best medicine, but unfortunately it's not available on prescription.

Germany – Early to bed, early to rise, makes a man healthy, wealthy and more likely to get a sun lounger.

- Holland – If the cap fits, you're safe.
- **Hollywood – Don't cross Lloyd Bridges till you come to him.**
- India – Beggars can't be avoided.
- **Ireland – Don't put the cart before the horse (actually, it's from an instruction manual).**
- Israel – Never buy a pig.
- **Italy – Accidents will happen in the best regulated families in Sicily.**
- Japan – Get rid of the scavenging birds before you bring the harvest in (rook before you reap).
- **Middle East – The pen is mightier than the sword, but the sword is more humane.**
- **North Africa – Once bitten, twice as likely to get rabies.**
- Norway – Never look a pissed Norse in the mouth.
- Rome – Milton Keynes *was* built in a day.
- **Russia – Don't put new wine into old Boris.**
- Russia (Chernobyl) – Two heads are better than one.
- **Scotland – Cleanliness is next to Inverness.**
  Scotland – He who pays the piper will be held personally responsible.
  Scotland – Where there's muck, there's rum and egg.
- Spain – There are plenty more fish in your sea.
  Spain – Never put all your Basques in one exit.
- Venice – You can't teach an old Doge new tricks.
- **Washington – Where there's a will, there's a whey-hey-hey!**

Historical Headlines

This is the popular round where the teams suggest how certain historical events might be reported in today's newspapers and periodicals. It's not to be confused with the old game "Historical Nedlines", where the players listen to a lengthy series of anecdotes by Ned Sherrin, the winner being the first to spot a living heterosexual ...

NELSON VICTORIOUS AT TRAFALGAR

- Daily Telegraph: Nelson Denies Selling Arm To Sierra Leone
- **Wrestling Times: Half Nelson Invented**
- Hello Magazine: What Emma Hamilton Will Be Wearing For That Funeral
- **Grecian Column Makers Monthly: New Work Likely**
- Guardian – Corrections & Clarifications page: Yesterday's headline should have read: Admiral Shot On Deck
- **Daily Mail: Nelson And Hardy – Gays In the Military – Where Will It End?**

THE GUNPOWDER PLOT

- The Daily Mail – Government Knives Out For Fawkes
- **The Star – Fuse What A Scorcher!**
- The Guardian – Remember, Remember, The Fourth Of November
- **The Sun – Guy Fawkes It Up●**
- Spiritualist's Weekly – Now There'll Be Fireworks
- **Exchange & Mart – Will swap eight barrels of gunpowder for one asbestos suit**
- The Financial Times – Boom Fails To Materialise

RICHARD III CROWNED KING AFTER PRINCES MURDERED IN TOWER

- Daily Express: Prince Murders – Police Are Following A Hunch
- **The Sun: Dick Head Crowned**
- Gloucester Echo: Local Man Gets Top Job
- **The Guardian: King Announces Winner Of Disco Tent**
- Labour Party Newsletter – Class Sizes Reduced In Royal Primary School
- **The Stage: Coronation Party – Children's Entertainers Axed At Last Minute**
- Exchange & Mart: King Willing To Swap Kingdom For Horse
- **The Sun: 10 Things You Never Knew About Richard III – 1. He Uses A Wok To Iron His Shirts**

KING HENRY VIII SPLITS WITH ROME

- Sunday Sport: Monasteries Dissolve – Actual Pictures!
- **The Guardian: Henry VIII Splits With Comb**
- Daily Telegraph: King Rejects Papal Bull, Gelatine And Tallow
- **The Stage: Jane Seymour Says "Stuff This, I'm Off To The States To Star In A Soap"**
- Daily Mail: Why The King Was Wrong by Paul Johnson on pages 8 and 9, 10, 11, 12, 13, 14 and 15
- **The Sun: Arriverderci Roma Says Horny Hal**
- Melody Maker: Greensleeves Composer On Top Of The Popes
- **London Evening Standard: Tube Strike Off**

Film Club

GARDENERS' FILM CLUB

Played while Samantha nipped down to the allotment to help a nice gentleman put fertiliser on his tomato plants (she was surprisingly keen to see his Gro-More in the potting shed)...

- The Lone Hydrangea
- **Back To The Fuschia starring Michael J Foxglove**
- The Loneliness Of The Long Distance Runner Bean
- **The Plums Of Navarone**
- The Compost Man Always Rings Twice
- **Driving Michaelmas Daisy**
- The Man Who Knew To Mulch directed by Albert Pitchfork
- **Gone With The Windowbox starring Lawn Green, Patrick Mower and Victor Manure**
- Sleeping With The Anenome
- **Clay Jones And The Temple Of Doom**
- The Bond classics: Greenfinger and Dr Hoe
- **Three Weedings and a Bonfire**
- Whose Afraid of Virginia Creeper
- **Primula, Queen of the Desert**
- Rebel Without A Cos
- **The Trowel of Oscar Wilde**
- The Great Train Shrubbery
- **Privets on Parade starring Petunia Clark, Robbie Cold Frame, Claire Bloom and Kate Bush (not to mention Graeme Garden)**
- A Manure For All Seasons
- **Laurel And Hardy Perennials**
- Gro Bag In Anger
- **Bring Me The Hedge Of Alfredo Garcia.**

HAIRDRESSERS' FILM CLUB

Played while Samantha nipped off to get her new bob to the length she prefers...

- Dye Hard starring the artist formerly known as Rinse
- **Toni & Guy's & Dolls**
- They Died With Their Roots Done
- **Not Too Much Off The Back To The Future**
- Mr Smith Goes To Wash 'N' Go
- **Rinse Tinge Tint**
- As Good As It Sets
- **Perms Of Endearment**
- Hair (the director's cut)
- **Top Bun**
- The Magnificent Salon
- **Quiff Vadis**
- The Color Purple
- **Barber Streisand in Funny Curl and A Star Is Shorn**
- Indiana Jones And The Last Pomade starring Shorn Completely and Hair-Extensions Ford
- **Mad Max Factor**
- No, No, Hairnet
- **The Lavender Hill Bob**
- Walt Disney's Peter Pan Tene Pro V Plus
- **And Bring Me The Head & Shoulders Of Alfredo Garcia.**

UNDERTAKERS' FILM CLUB

Played while Samantha slipped into the audience to check for signs of life...

- Robo Corpse
- **Far From The Madding Shroud**
- The Cremating Game
- **Cadavre Sixpence**
- Who Embalmed Roger Rabbit?
- **Gene Autry in Champion: The Wonder Hearse**
- Around The World In Eighty Graves by Necraphilias Fogg
- **Indiana Jones And The Chapel Of Rest**
- The Right Stiff
- **Walt Disney's 101 Cremations**
- Doctor Jekyl And Mr Formaldehyde
- **The Keystone Corpse**
- A Tomb With A View featuring the classic song about premature burial "I Hear You Knocking, But You Can't Get Out"
- **And Bring Me The Rest Of Alfredo Garcia.**

Late Arrivals at ...

THE SHAKESPEAREAN BALL

- Will you welcome, please, Mr and Mrs Arnot-Toby and their son, Toby Arnot-Toby.
- **And approaching now are a whole crowd of Russian girls – there's Tamara. And Tamara. And Tamara. Creeps!**
- All the way from Wales, there's Nigh Thera-Borrower and his girlfriend, Nora Lender-Bee.
- **Oh, look over there! There's George who's been sent by Godfrey, Harry and Anne. That's why you can hear everybody cry "Godfrey, Harry, Anne sent George".**
- Pray welcome the Balls-Myliege's and their son, Dennis Balls-Myliege.
- **There's someone very flashy – it's Bassanio. He's turned up in a Porsche.**

- There's just time to announce the results of the dancing competition. Now is the winner of our discotheque ...
- **I think that's Nonnie over there. I'll call her. Hey, Nonnie! No.**
- Ooh, there's a Bi-election result just coming in ... Loves! Labour's lost!
- **I'd like to warn all the guests to guard their puddings and watch out for Autolycus, whose "a snapper up of unconsidered trifles"... He's as tight as Andronicus.**
- Ah, here are the Things, with their unfortunate son who always has such a rough time in Scandinavia – Sam Thing, who's rotten in the State of Denmark.
- **And there's a Greek gentleman selling neckware – it's the Tie Man of Athens.**
- Oh, here's Stratford Johns and an Avon lady. Good Lord! Stratford's on Avon. Stop that!
- **Mr and Mrs Poor-Yorick and their daughter, Alice ... and she's brought her dog. Out, damn Spot!**
- Mr and Mrs Comparetheeto-Asummersday and their daughter, Shelley Comparetheeto-Asummersday.
- **And there's the Encrantz girl, I think. Rose Encrantz. No, I'm mistaken, it's a Rose by any other name.**

THE MUSICIANS' BALL

- First up, will you welcome please, Bill Oddie, and his son, Mel Oddie.
- **From Sweden, Mr and Mrs Night-of-the-Proms, and their son, Lars Night-of-the-Proms.**
- Will you welcome, Mr and Mrs Tone, and their son, Barry Tone, and his man, Dolin, who's a bit of a liar.
- **There's the freezer salesman, known to us all as Ice Ted Ford.**
- Will you greet the arrival of Mr and Mrs Harmonic-Orchestra, and their son, Phil Harmonic-Orchestra. And Albert Hall.
- **Mr and Mrs Uendo, and their none-too-bright son, dim Ian Uendo.**
- And there's that music revolutionary, Che Mber Music.
- **Oh, they've let Jo in, which is surprising as I thought they were going to ban Jo.**
- There's Hitler or some other German lieder.
- **From Italy, there are Signor and Signore É Mobile and their daughter, Donna – she's the Strumpet Voluntary.**
- Ah, there are the Blues Brothers with their wonderfully disgusting sister, Bad Penny.

- **The O'Nets and their daughter, Clarrie O'Net.**
- Mr and Mrs Sizer, and their daughter, Cynthia Sizer.
- **And will you welcome Mr and Mrs Ube, and their pornographer son, the blue Dan Ube.**
- And finally, welcome from Ireland, the O'Lyns, and their daughters, Vi and Mand O'Lyn.

Humph's Gazetteer of the British Isles

GUILDFORD It is not every Surrey commuter town that can boast not only a bustling Bohemian Latin Quarter but also a Moorish citadel surrounded by a warren of dark sinister streets that provided film locations for Truffaut, Fassbinder and Bergman, and neither can Guildford.

The town is first recorded in the 9th century, when King Alfred used Guildford as a base to launch his attack on Danish-held London, his army managing to reach the outskirts of the capital in less than six hours; a feat occasionally matched to this day by South West Trains.

The name "Guildford" derives from the old English "Golden Ford" and, when a new town was recently built nearby, tradition dictated it should be named in similar fashion and so became "Little Metallic Bronze Datsun on the Down".

Guildford really began to grow after the construction of the Wey Navigation Canal, providing 19th-century merchants with a means to distribute their products and 20th-century consumers with somewhere to dump their old ones.

In 1837, one Josiah Hawkins came here and built England's first-ever paper mill. Sadly, during the Great Gale of 1838, it blew away.

Nearby are many natural attractions, including Surrey's highest point at Leith Hill. Allowing for weather conditions, on a reasonable day you can see as far as Orpington. On a perfect day you can't see it all.

OXFORD is a delightful old city, famous for its Dreaming Spires, ancient colleges and regular bazaar, where visitors can browse and purchase all manner of silks, spices and rich tapestries, particularly after the arrival of the spring camel trains, swelling the indigenous population of the casbah with the merry chatter of Arab and Berber tongues. **(Editor's note: This account isn't strictly accurate, as the camel trains don't usually arrive until June, which is well after spring in these latitudes.)**

The name "Oxford" came about when an observant local noticed an ox in a ford and thought it would make a nice name for a university city. It is a sobering thought that had the animal in question been a cat, our greatest seat of learning would have been situated in a suburb of Lewisham. It is a charitable tradition of Oxford colleges that they provide public bath houses fed by natural cool water springs for the use of weary travellers. On a hot summer's day, there is nothing to beat popping into the college baths, stripping off and immediately feeling a little fresher.

WATFORD It was in the 11th Century that the Catalonian King Wilfred came upon a site by a water crossing, where he laid down the foundations of a new city which was to become the envy of Holy Roman Empire. With its ancient covered market, Romanesque brick towers inlaid with fine enamelled tiles, a Baroque Cathedral and a former Summer Palace, housing the finest collection of Renaissance artworks in Northern Europe, there are few things finer than to spend an afternoon browsing amidst its remarkable Gothic splendour; a legacy

owed to that Great King Wilfred of Catalonia. What a pity he never visited Watford.

Modern Watford is associated with glamour, high finance and the international jet-set, all exemplified by the town's most famous son: Nick Leeson. Located on one of the most ancient thoroughfares out of London, Watford is the first place you come to on the way to wherever it is you're really going.

WINDSOR gave its name to a type of chair, a knot and – most famously – a soup, although this was before the Royal Borough changed its name from "Campbell's Cream of Mushroom-on-Thames". But a stone's throw across the river is Eton, with its world-renowned school. A browse through the school records reveals that: "Famous Old Etonians include the Duke of Wellington, William Gladstone, George Orwell and Humphrey Lyttelton, the jazz musician and panel game chairman". Curiously, they don't record what those first three were famous for.

Windsor has a proud association with the Royal Family. It was in 1917 that the House of Saxe-Coburg Gotha took their new name from the place where they loved to spend so much of their time. By the same tradition, when the young Sarah Ferguson married Prince Andrew, she naturally assumed the title "Duchess of Airport".

For the finest view of Windsor Castle, it is best approached through "Henry VIII's Gateway" which, thanks to a recent merger, is now officially known as "Henry VIII's Budgens".

A short journey out of town takes you to Windsor Safari Park where, if you're lucky, you may glimpse a pride of lions in search of wildebeest migrating south across the vast plains of the Thames Valley. You might also like to pay a visit to the successful new "Legoland" theme park next door. For a small fee, parents can take their children to enjoy a large area of toy buildings constructed out of plastic bricks. Alternatively, they can save their money and take the kids to Milton Keynes for the day.

Book Club

HOSPITAL BOOK CLUB

*Played while the teams suggested books
likely to make suitable reading in hospital.
Samantha was off with a team of
paramedics. They were so excited at the
thought, they just couldn't wait for her to
arrive so they could get their ambulance and
stretcher out for the evening.*

- Enema Of The People
- **The Forceps Saga by John Gallbladder**
- Lady Chatterley's Liver
- **Paddy Doyle Ha Ha Ha You Can Put Your Trousers Back On Now**
- Colon the Barbarian
- **Catheter Come Home**
- Cystitis Andronicus
- **The Rectum's Wife**
- Popeye the Say Ah Man
- **Diarrhoea Of A Nobody**
- Emily Brontë's Worrying Bites
- **The Honorary Tonsil**
- Up Stethoscope
- **The Greatest Suppository Ever Sold**
- Bleak Arse
- **Hernia Shrunk The Kidneys**
- Cold Compress Farm
- **The C S Lewis omnibus featuring The Chronicles of Hernia**
- Bridget Jones's Diarrhoea
- **Dial M For Matron**
- Madame Ovary
- **From the Ian Fleming canon: Coldfinger, Dr No!, Thunderbowl and For Your Thighs Only**
- Captain Corelli's Lanolin
- **John Pilgrim's The Bunion's Progress**
- The Stitches of Salem
- **Anaesthesia Karenina**
- The Viagra Story – Hard Times
- **Stump Collecting For Boys**
- The Queen Mother's favourite: Goodbye Mr Hips
- **Womb With A View**
- Cool Hand Luke
- **Back Passage To India**
- Great Expectorations
- **How Gangrene Was My Valley**
- The Clockwork Syringe
- **Around The Ward In Eighty Days**
- George Orwell's 98.4
- **Fatal Traction**
- For the Department of Urology: On Golden Pond
- **And outside the Haemorrhoid ward: Coriolanus and The Ipcress Pile**
- From Here To Maternity
- **And anything with an appendix**

Historical Postcards

Without these eye-witness messages from famous historical events we'd have been left ignorant of many of the shifting frontiers of human knowledge. For example, it's thanks to only a few lines on a postcard that we know precisely how Admiral Horatio Wellington was inspired to invent the steam telegraph when he observed a sandwich falling from a tree, at which point he jumped out of the bath shouting "Ulrika!".

- **Neville Chamberlain from Munich:**
  Weather good. Hitler charming.
  Piece of paper follows.

- **Three Wise Men from Orient:**
  Off to see new Messiah, who's just been born. Bit of a bummer what with it all happening on Christmas Day.

- **From Pompeii:**
  Vesuvius erupted last night.
  We were all petrified.

- **Paul to friends in Corinth from Damascus:**
  Having a blinding time.
  Long letter to follow.

- **Jane Austen to mother from Bath:**
  Publisher loves *Pride and Prejudice* but says all the f-ing and blinding has to go.

- **Florence Nightingale from the Crimea:**
  Dear Matron, All a terrible mistake. In my letter I said I wanted to go to the cinema.

- **Dr Livingstone from the Congo:**
  Dear All, What a laugh this is. Stanley turned up again today. This time I hid behind the mud huts.

- **Mrs Julius Caesar from Disneyland:**
  Dear Caez, Place full of ghastly children. Wish you were Herod.

- **Kipling from India:**
  Weather exceedingly good. Beaches exceedingly good. Nightlife exceedingly good. Cake crap.

POST CARD

BEAGLES POST CARDS

BEST IN THE WORLD

Working flat out. Pope now wants something more like the opening titles to "The South Bank Show". Am in agony, but the ecstasy keeps me going.

Michaelangelo

Sistine Chapel, Rome

- **Captain Scott from the Antarctic:**
  The weather's not up to much. Catering poor. Oates is just popping out to post this now.

- **King Harold from Hastings:**
  Hastings lovely. Looking forward to the big day. Not sure if we should have booked the Red Arrows.

- **From George Stevenson on Rocket during inaugural trip from Stockton to Darlington:**
  Hi. I'm on the train. I'll talk to you later.

- **Julius Caesar to his wife Portia from Londinium:**
  Hail Portia. Vici, vidi, veni – or vice versa. Status quo good. Beatles better. Hail and Pace. Julius

- **Nelson to Lady Hamilton from Trafalgar:**
  Having a great time at Trafalgar, apart from the pigeons. Captain Hardy has shown me great loyalty and affection, though I still have to remind him "no tongues". Can't wait to be back with you – hope the eye and the arm are enough to be going on with.

- **Captain Cook from Botany Bay:**
  Dear Sir. Have introduced cricket to the aborigines. Close of play on first day: England all out 48, Aborigines 743 for 2. Have you thought of turning Yorkshire into a penal settlement?

- **Hannibal from the Alps:**
  This is the last time I charter a jumbo from Virgin.

Connection Quiz

If asked to link "a £2,000 bribe to a prostitute", "accusations of insider dealing" and "huge contributions to Party funds", you might make the connection that none of these things prevented Jeffrey Archer from being awarded a peerage. Here's a game where the teams have to identify the cunningly concealed connection linking certain people or things ...

Q. What's the connection between a bottle of Head & Shoulders, Ian Paisley and The European Community?
A. Both Paisley and Head & Shoulders have had a run-in with the EC because a new EU ruling has come out that Head & Shoulders has to change its name because the bottles don't contain any head or shoulders, or at least not very much, and the town of Paisley has had to change its name for fear of being confused with Dr Ian Paisley. The town will now be known as Noisy Bigot.
(*Ans. Irish men suffer less from dandruff than any other European community.*)

Q. What connects Bruce Willis, Charles I and Winston Churchill?
A. Bruce Willis was in the film *Die Hard*. Charles I died pretty hard and Winston Churchill died hard of hearing.
(*Ans. They were all stutterers. Bruce Willis and Winston Churchill had their stutters cured by therapy, whereas Charles I underwent major surgery.*)

Q. What's the connection between Ordinary, Boring and Dismal?
A. They're Snow White's reserves.
(*Ans. They're all places in America.*)

Q. What's the connection between a guinea pig, the Duke of Edinburgh and 1st Degree Burns?
A. The connection is what they're not. You can't get a pig for a guinea, the Duke of Edinburgh doesn't come from Edinburgh and Burns didn't go to University – he was a farm labourer.
(*Ans. Prince Philip is Patron of the Guinea Pig Club treating airmen suffering from burns.*)

Q. What connects Ryan Giggs, William Shakespeare and Karl Marx?
A. Ryan Giggs and Karl Marx are both left wingers and Shakespeare played for Stratford United.
(*Ans. They all took their mothers' surnames. If they hadn't, they would have been Ryan Wilson, William Arden and Karl Pressburg.*)

Q. What connects moving into a new home, squeezing a pimple and old age?

A. They all necessitate new carpets.

(Ans. They were all cited by the 18th-century French physician, Jean Esquirol, as the three most likely causes of madness.)

Q. What connects Coco Chanel, Herbert Hoover, Boris Karloff and the prophet Mohammed?

A. They all gave their names to products: Coco Chanel – the popular bedtime drink, Herbert Hoover of course invented the Herbert Dab, Boris Karloff's real name was Lillet, and I won't risk a fatwa by going any further.

(Ans. They were all orphans.)

Q. What connects Gandhi, Napoleon and Sigmund Freud?

A. Napoleon said "An army marches on its stomach" and Gandhi said "I've had nothing in my stomach since March", while Sigmund Freud was listening.

(Ans. They all suffered from constipation.)

Q. What connects A, U, O and Y?

A. They're all lines in *The Archers*.

(Ans. They are the four shortest place names in the world. "A" is in Norway, "U" is in the Caroline Islands. "O" is in Japan and "Y" is in France.)

Q. What connects Dolly Parton, St Francis Of Assisi and Horatio Nelson?

A. Assisi has two eyes, Nelson had one eye and, if you're not careful, Dolly Parton could have your eye out.

(Ans. They were all under 5 foot 6 inches high.)

Q. What connects the Duke of Edinburgh and a dining room table?

A. Of late there have been rumours that they could be the parents of Prince Charles, who has the sensitivity of a dining room table and the same legs.

(Ans. The Duke of Edinburgh was born on a dining room table.)

Q. What connects the Sea Bass, the Land Snail and Danny La Rue?

A. They're all cross-dressers, particularly the land snail, which leaves a rather enticing trail of silver lamé wherever it goes.

(Ans. They all undergo transformations from males into females.)

Translations

As we develop ever closer relations with our European partners, it's worth noting that skill with a foreign tongue will always help you get on abroad. Another useful asset is an ability to translate some of the many foreign words and phrases that crop up increasingly in our own English language ...

A cappella The band hasn't turned up.

Ad hoc Liven up your rice pudding with a little German wine.

Ad nauseam The latest Benetton campaign.

Annus horribilis Do you mind if I don't sit down?

Après midi d'une faune You've been on the phone since lunch.

Après ski Plaster of Paris *or* I've finished the yoghurt.

Au clair de la lune Claire's a bit of a nutter.

Avant garde Next to last coach on the train.

Avez-vous faimes? Would you like my sister?

Bauhaus Dog kennel.

Beaujolais Nouveau Unsuitable for drinking.

Belle époque A cheap cut of pig meat.

Bidet Two days before D–Day.

Bona fide That's a genuine dog.

Bonsai Dyslexic kamikaze pilot.

Bratwürst Macaulay Culkin.

Bureau de change Superman's telephone box.

Cannelloni al forno Al's fallen in the canal.

Carpe diem Fish of the Day.

C'est la guerre Jumble sale.

Chacun à son goût Oh, you like Pot Noodle, do you?

Charabancs The cleaning lady's a goer.

Ciabatta The Wookie in *Star Wars*.

Cinquecento 100-year-old Chinaman.

Con allegro A second-hand car salesman.

Crèche A car accident in Woking.

Cul de sac My bag is in the refrigerator.

Daiwoo Host of *Supermarket Sweep*.

Dieu Et Mon Droit Margaret Thatcher's family motto: *God And Me Are Right*.

Donna è mobile A portable kebab stand.

Donna und blitzen The after-effects of a kebab.

Dossier Someone who sleeps under the bridges of Paris.

Droit de seigneur The gents is on the right.

Eldorado Didn't seem like a good idea in the beginning.

Ersatz A Somerset milliner.

Et in Arcadia ego I had an omelette down the shopping precinct.

Et tu Brute Blimey, you've splashed it all over and no mistake.

Eureka! BO!

Fiat lux Car wash.

Film noir Oh, damn! The holiday photos haven't come out.

Fin de siècle Bicycle lover.

Graffiti Newton's Law of Dyslexia.

Grand Prix Michael Winner.

Hande hoch! The white wine is at your elbow!

Hara-kiri An opera singer educated at public school.

Have a nice day! Now bugger off!

Hors d'oeuvre Ladies who hang around diesel pumps.

Ich bin ein Berliner I am a misprint for a bin liner.

Ich Dien I am Jayne Torville's dancing partner.

Ich liebe dich I'm very fond of Richard.

Infra dig I'm an archaeologist.

In loco parentis Engine driver.

Jihad What fundamentalist cowboys yell.

La belle dame sans merci The operator never says "Thank you".

Magnum opus Tom Selleck's Irish cat.

Masseuse A roomful of stutterers.

Mens sana in corpore sano Corporal punishment is available in the men's sauna.

Mi kaza tu kaza My house has two lavatories.

Moi aussi I am an Australian.

Non compos mentis I don't think that's meant to be fertiliser.

O Sole Mio That's my fish.

Paterfamilias A well-known comedy routine.

Petite chose Your flies are open.

Prima Donna Sean Penn's bachelor days.

Sang froid I'm dreaming of a white Christmas.

Sic Transit Gloria Mundi Gloria was sick in the van, but she'll be in on Monday.

Snickers Spanties.

Soupçon Dinner's nearly ready.

Spaghetti carbonara My dinner's on fire.

Steak tartare The meat's off.

Sub judice The Israeli Underground System.

Tant pis, tant mieux Auntie's been to the bathroom and she's feeling much better now.

Trompe d'oeil Ooh, that one made my eyes water.

Tutti frutti Baked beans.

Valpolicella Mr Doonican's parrot is in the string section.

Veni, vidi, vici I came to see Vicky; unfortunately she was suffering from a social disease.

Vin ordinaire Ford transit.

Songbook

BARBERS

Played after Samantha was called back to the salon, where a regular client was waiting to have his length adjusted before she finished him off with an expert blow ...

- I Can Feel It Combing In The Air At Night
- **Thank Heaven Follicle Girls**
- Bar-Bar-Bar Bar-Barber-Ann by The Bleach Boys
- **Dandruff Keeps Falling Off My Head**
- Shave Your Missus For Me
- **I Dyed It My Way**
- I Spray A Little Hair For You
- **Shorn In The USA by Mousse Springsteen**
- Oh Yes, I'm The Great Split Ender
- **The Blue Rinse Mountains Of Virginia by Loreal and Hardy**
- Kiss Curl by the Artist Formerly Known As Rinse
- **Never Mind The Forelocks**
- Condition Yourself At Home
- **Highlights Coiffeur Highlights Tea**
- Tinted Love by Soft Gel
- **Give My Hairpiece A Chance**
- What's The Story Crowning Glory
- **Sonny With The Fringe On Top**
- Parting Is Such Sweet Sorrow
- **And anything by Quiff Richard.**

WEIGHTWATCHERS

Played while Samantha popped off to check out how well-equipped her new gym was ...

- I'll Never Get Over You
- **Me And My Girth**
- Once In Royal Obee City
- **A Weigh-in A Manger**
- Lurpak Be A Lady Tonight
- **The Son Has Got His Fat On**
- My Sweet Lard
- **Chubby, Chubby, Cheek, Cheek**
- Reach Out And I'll Be There, There and There
- **When I'm 64-64-64**
- Strawberry Flans Forever by The Flab Four
- **I Who Have Stuffing by Burly Chassis**
- I'm Being Followed By A Huge Shadow by Fat Stephens
- **I Talk To My Knees**
- Two Lips Like Amsterdam
- **Gladys Knight and the Hips**
- When The Red Red Robin Goes Flob Flob Flobbin' Along
- **50 Ways To Lose Your Blubber**
- You're Once, Twice, Three Times A Lady
- **Do You Know The Weight Of Sam Hosé?**
- By The Cellulite Of The Silvery Moon.

PENSIONERS

Played after Samantha had nipped off to help the old man next door, who was having trouble using his stairlift. Every night she would put him on downstairs and then have to pull him off on the landing ...

- You Say "Tomatoes" And I Say "Eh?"
- **Another One Bites The Crust**
- When I Was 64
- **Stairlift To Heaven**
- Hit Me With Your Walking Stick
- **Da Ya Think I'm 60?**
- I Remember Who?
- **The Hippy Hippy Replacement**
- I Can't See Clearly Now
- **I'll Be Your Grey Haired Lover With Liver Pills**
- Wide-eyed And Legless with Hot Chocolate
- **I'm Forever Blowing Bubbles**
- Gimme Sheltered Accommodation
- **Twist And Gout**
- I Heard It Through The Deaf Aid
- **Shake Rattle and Roam**
- We're All Going On A Saga Holiday
- **Pappa's Got A Brand New Bag**
- I'm Putting In My Top Set
- **Eh? You're adorable! Eh? You're so beautiful. Eh?**
- Pump Up The Volume
- **Can't Get Used To Sluicing You**
- You've Lost That Lovin' Feeling by the Arthrighteous Brothers
- **There'll Be Blue Rinse Over The White Hair Of Dover**
- Rainy Night In Bournemouth
- **All I Want Is A Rheumatologist**
- The Incontinental
- **There Ain't No Cure For The Zimmer Frame Blues**
- Help!
- **I Can See Clearly Now The Specs Have Come**
- Baby, Will You Light The Fire
- **Itsy Bitsy Teeny Weenie Yellow Polka Dot Thermals**
- And Stayin' Alive.

Sound Charades

Our adaptation of the classic TV show *Give Us A Clue*, where the chairman gave players a card with a book, play or film title to mime against the clock. And what fun it was! Who will ever forget the sparkle in Lionel Blair's eye as he received *Free Willy* from Michael Aspel for two minutes? Or when Una Stubbs, her hands a blur, managed *Three Men In A Boat* in less than 90 seconds. Here are some more to try at home ...

TV PROGRAMME – THREE WORDS

THE QUEEN: Philip?

PRINCE PHILIP: Yes, Bessie?

THE QUEEN: One doesn't quite know how to put this ...

PRINCE PHILIP: Spit it out, woman.

THE QUEEN: On your head ... there's something crawling about.

PRINCE PHILIP: Well, swat it.

THE QUEEN: One's only got one's handbag.

PRINCE PHILIP: Get on with it.

(SOUND EFFECT: THUD!)

PRINCE PHILIP: Ow, that hurt one.

THE QUEEN: Well, one's done the trick now.

(Wildlife On One)

FILM – THREE WORDS

VOICE 1: Where's that fireplace gone?

VOICE 2: I'm sorry, it's my fault. I forgot to lock the living room door.

(The Great Escape)

FILM AND BOOK - FOUR WORDS

MAN 1: Oh, excuse me ...

MAN 2: What's that?

MAN 1: Excuse me?

MAN 2: It's about quarter past four.

MAN 1: I simply wanted ...

MAN 2: Pardon?

MAN 1: I just wanted to tell you ...

MAN 2: I'm sorry, I can't hear you. I've got a banana in my ears.

MAN 1: I just wanted to tell you – it's not a banana.

(Prick Up Your Ears)

STAGE SHOW - ONE WORD

VOICE 1: Oh, what can we do? We've booked Torville and Dean, and the ice has melted.

(Riverdance)

TV PROGRAMME - ONE WORD

VOICE 1: What's that then? There on your arm?

VOICE 2: It's a "Snight".

VOICE 1: You don't see many of those. Is it an antique or what?

VOICE 2: No, it's not antique, it's not second hand. I just got it this morning.

VOICE 1: You never.

VOICE 2: I did. I went down the Snight shop, I said "Give me a fresh one", and by chance they had one in.

VOICE 1: It's very impressive. Hold it up to the light.

VOICE 2: You ought to get yourself one of these.

VOICE 1: I certainly will.

VOICE 2: You're never alone with a Snight

(Newsnight)

Postbag

FROM THE SECRETARY GENERAL OF THE RHYL AND DISTRICT PSYCHIC INSOMNIACS TRUST:

Dear Mr Littlejohn,

I know what you're thinking. Many heartfelt thanks to you and the teams for all the help you've given our members, many of whom hadn't slept a wink in years before discovering your programme.

Yours faithfully,

Mrs Trellis,

North Wales.

ON HEARING EXCITING NEWS:

Dear Libby,

Many congratulations to the teams. I've just read the exciting news that Graeme, Tim and Barry have been offered long term contracts to appear exclusively on Sky. And hats off also to the Highlands & Islands Development Board for giving them the chance!

Yours faithfully,

Mrs Trellis,

North Wales

A TELEGRAM RECEIVED DURING THE OFF SEASON:

DEAR YEHUDI STOP
WHEN DOES NEW SERIES START STOP
WITH NEW WALKMAN RADIO CAN
LISTEN ON TOP OF BUS STOP ENJOY
SHOW SO MUCH OFTEN DON'T
NOTICE BUS STOP AT STOP STOP
HOWEVER, FIND GAMES A BIT STOP
START STOP.
TRELLIS MRS N WALES PS AS EVER
CAN'T WAIT TO HEAR THE TEAMS'
SINGING STOP

IN RESPONSE TO OUR *I'M SORRY I HAVEN'T A CLUE* AUDIENCE RESPONSE SURVEY:

We asked 20,000 listeners to rate their level of satisfaction with the show: "excellent", "good", or merely "well above average". The reply we received came from a Mrs Trellis of North Wales, who marked the following boxes:

NEITHER GOOD NOR BAD	☑
POOR	☑
VERY POOR	☑
EXTREMELY POOR	☑
WORDS BEGIN TO FAIL ME AS TO QUITE HOW POOR	☑
BUTTOCK-CLENCHINGLY PISS-POOR	☑

(Editor's note: In fact, Mrs Trellis sent us the wrong form, but we'll be happy to forward it as soon as someone at Virgin Rail sends us their address.)

One Song to the Tune of Another

Using the description of a game as its title still goes on in some countries, particularly China. Literally translated, the Chinese for snooker is "use thin rod to clear table of coloured balls"; skating is translated as "catch frostbite while falling off metal shoes" and rugby is translated as "push face into buttocks of man in front", which coincidentally is also the title of the new BBC management training manual. Here are the top 20 "Songs To The Tune Of Others" specially compiled by Gallup ...

1. "The Laughing Policeman" to the tune of "As Time Goes By".
2. **"Come Into The Garden, Maud" to the tune of "Chitty Chitty Bang Bang".**
3. Madonna's "Hanky Panky" to the tune of "Land Of Hope And Glory".
4. **"My Old Man's A Dustman" to the tune of "Heartbreak Hotel".**
5. Marvyn Gaye's "Sexual Healing" to the tune of "Two Little Boys".
6. **"A Whiter Shade Of Pale" to the tune of "My Old Man's A Dustman".**
7. "Oh, What A Beauty" to the tune of "The Sunshine Of Your Smile".
8. **"Hit Me With Your Rhythm Stick" to the tune of "O Sole Mio".**
9. "Where Did You Get That Hat?" to the theme from *The Dam Busters*.
10. **"I've Got A Loverly Bunch Of Coconuts" to the theme from *Swan Lake*.**

11. "Gilly Gilly Ossenfeffer Katzenellen Bogen By The Sea" to the tune of "The William Tell Overture".
12. **"Great Balls of Fire" to the tune of "The Blue Danube".**
13. "Pinball Wizard" to the tune of "Jerusalem".
14. **"Knees Up, Mother Brown" to the tune of "Sailing By".**
15. Harry Nilsson's "Without You" to the tune of "The Can Can".
16. **"Wild Thing" to the tune of "Memory".**
17. "Old MacDonald Had A Farm" to the tune of "New York, New York".
18. **"Me And Mrs Jones" to the tune of Aled Jones's "Walking In The Air".**
19. "Wannabe" by the Spice Girls to the tune of "Model Of A Modern Major General".
20. **"Love Me Tender" to the theme from the Archers.**

Humph's Gazetteer
of the British Isles

BURY ST EDMUNDS This historic Suffolk town is swelled to overflowing during the annual carnival, when thousands of gaily-clad, olive-skinned dancers Samba through the streets to the incessant rhythmic beat of the bongo. Towards dawn, the heaving throng form into a torch-lit procession which wends its way up nearby Sugar Loaf Mountain to watch the sun rise over Copacabana Beach, their huge, feathered headdresses

swaying in the warm tropical breeze as they chant and sing their welcome to the new dawn. These are just a few of the rich pleasures which make this town unmistakably Bury St Edmunds. Or is that Rio de Janeiro?

Bury St Edmunds also became famous recently following a promotional campaign run by the Suffolk Tourist Board. There was mass rioting in the streets when, thanks to an unfortunate printing error, thousands of posters were issued encouraging one and all to "VISIT SUFFOLK AND BURY NOEL EDMONDS". One can only imagine their disappointment.

CAMBRIDGE is the university city that has a special place in our hearts, as it is here that Tim Brooke-Taylor and Graeme Garden were discovered when they were under graduates. Luckily they slipped away in the confusion of the police raid and no charges were ever brought. Barry Cryer was also once offered a chair here. How thoughtful of the old lady to give up her seat on the bus.

Other great historical Cambridge names include Sir Isaac Newton, who was Professor of Gravitational Physics at Trinity, where he also taught a little Greek. The little Greek, incidentally, went on to open Cambridge's premier moussaka bar.

At nearby Grantchester lives the novelist, Conservative peer and stock market Mystic Meg, Jeffrey Archer. Archer upholds that fine tradition of English writing that can be traced in a direct line from Webster's dramatic quill, through Swift's satirical pen, right down to his own overworked photocopier.

CANTERBURY is an historic cathedral city and weekend residence of the Archbishop, who at other times lives at Lambeth Palace. Archbishops have for centuries made annual pilgrimages on foot all the way from South London to Canterbury, all the while singing "Onward Christian Soldiers", "Jerusalem" and of course the piece written specially for the journey "Doing the Lambeth Walk, Oi!".

Canterbury has been the inspiration for many works of literature. The best known must be the tales of Chaucer's Pilgrims, but of course T S Eliot was also stirred by the tragic story of Thomas à Becket to write his "Old Possum's Book of Practical Cathedral Murders". With its Marlowe Theatre and Marlowe Exhibition, Canterbury will always be connected with

the mysterious Marlowe too, though quite why Raymond Chandler should have based his LA gum shoe private detective stories in South-East England is even more of a mystery.

Canterbury is set deep in the Kentish rolling green countryside, for centuries referred to as the "Garden of England". However, with the new direct rail link to Brussels from nearby Ashford, Kent has become known as the "Patio of Belgium".

The carving of the Eurostar link through the county's rich agricultural land was the cause of much controversy at the time but now, with the benefit of hindsight, we are beginning to see the undoubted benefits of rail links with the continent. Parisians can now hail a taxi in the Champs Elysee or the Rue Montmartre to the Gard du Nord at 11 a.m., speed their way effortlessly at 130 mph through the tunnel before noon, and by two o'clock be stuck at a points failure just outside Orpington.

Abbreviations

With the pace of modern life, it's much more convenient to abbreviate whenever you can. The added bonus is that no one will understand what you are saying. Here are some interesting examples used to test the teams ...

- **AAAA** The Society For The Deaf
  (*Ans. American Association for the Advancement of Atheism*)
- **BFMF** Bruce Forsyth's Matt Finish
  (*Ans. British Footwear Manufacturer's Federation*)
- **CIEC** Campaign for the Impregnation of Edwina Curry
  (*Ans. Centre Internationale D'Étude Criminologique*)
- **COPEC** Colin On Piano Empties Concert halls
  (*Ans. Christian Order of Politics, Economics and Citizenship*)
- **CSK** Keep Spelling Correct
  (*Ans. Campaign for Safe Kitchens*)
- **CSRHH** The Conservative Sisterhood For The Re-election Of Herr Hitler
  (*Ans. The Campaign For The Safe Return Of Humph's Hooter*)
- **DELTA** Dave Eric Lee Travis Actually
  (*Ans. Detailed Labour and Time Analysis*)
- **LLAAII** It's an abbreviation for: "Sorry Darling, The Car's Broken Down" (as in "'Ell, 'Ell, AA, Aye, Aye")
  (*Ans. Le Altesse Imperiale*)

- **LLAARR** An abbreviation for: "Sorry Darling, The Car's Broken Down in Somerset"
  (*Ans. Le Altesse Royale*)
- **MSUL** Marks & Spencer's Underwear Leaks
  (*Ans. Medical Schools of the University of London*)
- **NFMPS** National Front Medieval Poetry Society
  (*Ans. National Federation of Master Printers In Scotland*)
- **PASMA** Pass Arthur Scargill's Money Around
  (*Ans. Prefabricated Aluminium Scaffold Manufacturers Association*)
- **RFCMC** Radio 4 Can Murder Comedy
  (*Ans. Reconstruction Finance Commission of Monte Carlo*)
- **TDIA** Tim's Done It Again
  (*Ans. The Tropical Disease Investigation Agency*)
- **WAMDT** Women Against Men Dangling Things
  (*Ans. Women Against Media Distortion of the Truth*)

Euro TV and Radio Guide

With the ever-closer links we are forging with our European neighbours, it's no surprise that the *I'm Sorry I Haven't A Clue* teams are so frequently being invited to perform overseas – by listeners to the programme in Britain. And as European popular culture increasingly mirrors our own, it's interesting to note the number of Euro TV and radio programmes that bear a striking resemblance to our own ...

- Albania – One Man And King Zog
- **Austria – Dr Finlay's Kitsbuehl**
- Belgium – Ostenders

  Belgium – Have I Got Bruges For You
- Brussels – EU And Yours
- **Denmark – Today's The Dane**

  Denmark – Blind Dane
- **Dublin – This Is Your Liffey**
- Eastern Europe – Michael Palin Presents

  Poland To Poland

  Eastern Europe – Crimewatch Ukraine

  Eastern Europe – They Think It's Moldavia
- France – Re-run of Alsace & Gaiters

  France – Encore L'Addition (that's just a repeat of The Bill)

  France – One Man And His Frog

  France – The Aix Files

  France – The Monet Programme

  France – Devil's Island Discs

  France – Can Cook, Will Cook

  France – Call My Boeuf

- Germany – Ve Ask Ze Questions Time

  Germany – The Cologne Ranger (and his Horst Wessel)

  Germany – The Big Bratwürst (with Leipzig and Zag)

  Germany – Whose Rhine Is It Anyway?

  Germany – Panzer's People

  Germany – Birds of A Führer

  Germany – Reich To Reply

  Germany – London's Burning has been renamed The Good Old Days

  Germany – Never Mind The Buzzbombs

  Germany – It Ain't 'Alf Dortmund

  Germany – Baden-Badeners Question Time

  Germany – Friday Night Is Munich Night

  Germany – They Think It's Hanover

  Germany – The Old Horst Wessel Test

  Germany – They tried Michael Buerk's 999 but it was a no-no-no... but they did enjoy Magnus Magnusson with Master Race

- **Greece - Have Hypotenuse For You**
- Holland – Wim'll Fix It
  Holland - Bols Eye
  Holland – One Man And His Clog
- **Ireland - One Man And His Bog**
  Ireland – The Archers is now on eight nights a week
- **Israel - They Think It's Passover**
- Italy – Rome And Away
  Italy - Popular sitcom called Men Behaving Normally
- Netherlands – Supermaastricht Sweep with Dale Windmill
- **Norway - One Man And His Log**
  Norway – Only Trolls and Norses
- **Poland - National Zlottery Live**
  Poland – Torville & Dean in Let's Face The Music And Gdansk
- **Portugal - Lisbon With Mother**
- Romania – Bucharest At Bedtime
- **Russia - Have I Got Queues For You?**
  Russia – Shooting Tsars
- **Scandinavia - Inspector Norse**
  Scandinavia – Two Finn Ladies
- **Scotland - Have I Got Troos For You?**
- Spain – Flog The Dead Donkey
  Spain - The World At Juan
- Switzerland – Emmenthal Farm

Switzerland - has combined World At War with The Money Programme
Switzerland – Ready Steady Cuckoo and Heidi Hi
- **Turkey - Challenge Ankara**
- Venice – One Man & His Doge
- **Yugoslavia - Croatian Street**
  Yugoslavia – Montenegro's Flying Serbians
  Yugoslavia - I'm Sarajevo A Clue
  Yugoslavia – Are You Being Serbed?

Late Arrivals at ...

THE VICARS' BALL

- Please welcome first, Mr and Mrs Collar, and their son, Doug Collar.
- **Also here tonight is the Right Honourable Charles Ismae-Shepherd and his father, the Lord Ismae-Shepherd.**
- Mr and Mrs Nod, and their son, Si Nod.
- **A strange couple from the Church now: It's an abbot and a beadle, who've formed an unholy alliance to produce *Beadle's Abbot*.**
- Will you also greet Benny Dictus, Jenny Fleckt, Dai O'Sease, Ann Glican-Church, and, on her own, Penny Tential.
- **It's Cabaret time now and we've got a parade of knickerless parsons. They're all standing in a line, they'll get a queue-rate! Good job, I brought my Rev counter.**
- Mr and Mrs Ologist and their effeminate bell-ringing son, Camp Ian Ologist.
- **Mr and Mrs Meek, and their saintly son, blessed Arthur Meek.**
- Also, Mr and Mrs Ayshon-of-the-Magi and their son, Theodore Ayshon-of-the-Magi.
- **Stand and greet Mr and Mrs Rendeth-the-lesson and their son, Andy Rendeth-the-lesson.**
- And finally, Mr and Mrs Ment and their newt, Esther Ment.

THE ORNITHOLOGISTS' BALL

- Please welcome first, all the way from Israel, Mr and Mrs Neagle and their daughter, Golda.
- **Mr and Mrs Tit and their son, Tom.**
- From Wales, the family Mott with their mining son, Black Willie.
- **Mr and Mrs Cann and their footballing son, Pelé.**
- Mr and Mrs Shag and their children, who are far too numerous to mention.
- **From Germany, Mr and Mrs Ingull, that's Frau and Herr Ingull.**
- From Ireland, Mr and Mrs O'Warbler and their son, Will O'Warbler.

- **Mr and Mrs Tross and their peripatetic son, the Wandering Albert Tross.**
- Mr and Mrs Urns and their none-too-well-endowed son, Little Bit.
- **From Spain, Mr and Mrs Pretty-Boy-Then and their son, José Pretty-Boy-Then.**
- From the Berkeley Square region, Mr and Mrs Gale and their son, Newton.
- **Bad news for the grouse, here comes Gloria Stwelfth.**
- From Scotland, Mr and Mrs Douting-Toslimbridge and their son, Wee Ken Douting-Toslimbridge.
- **And finally, there's Mr and Mrs Red-Breast and their son, Arthur.**

SANTA'S CHRISTMAS BALL

- Will you welcome first, please, Mr and Mrs L Toe and their daughter, Miss L Toe – oh and there's somebody under her.
- **Pray silence and loosen your beards for Mr and Mrs Tide-Logs and their bald son, Yul.**
- And will you welcome Mr and Mrs Amanger and their son, Wayne.
- **From Wales, will you be appreciative of Mr and Mrs Arnot-Included and their intellectually challenged son, Batty Rhys Arnot-Included.**
- Will you welcome, please, Mr and Mrs Ivy and their son, the bishop – the Holy Andy Ivy.
- **From Mexico, Mr and Mrs Horse-Opensleigh and their son, Juan.**
- Another crisis! I've heard that Santa's drunk and he's holding a painting by a French 18th Century pastoral artist and a piece of paper out of a cracker. Oh no! He's blotto in the grotto with a Watteau and a motto.
- **And finally, a very big welcome please for Mr and Mrs Even and their pizza-making son – yes, it's Deep Pan Crispian Even.**

Historical Headlines

In the olden days, before newspapers were invented, the only news came from someone called a town crier, who went into the market square and shouted out the main news stories before putting an enormous chequerboard on his back so people could do the crossword. Here are more of the teams' suggestions of how today's newspapers and periodicals might have reported certain historical events ...

ASSASSINATION OF JULIUS CAESAR

- The Daily Mirror: Julius Caesar Is Ides Victim
- **The Rome Standard: Omnia Caesar In Tres Partes Divisa Est**
- Lancashire Evening Post: Mark Anthony Comes To Bury
- **The Independent: Mark Anthony Asks For Ear Loans**
- The Daily Star: Yon Cassius Has A Lean And Hungry Look – Is It Bulimia?
- **Tailor & Cutter: Sketchleys Opens New Branch In Rome**
- The Guardian – Corrections & Clarifications page: Yesterday's headline should have read "Caesar Slayed" not "Caesar Salad"

SIR WALTER RALEIGH PRESENTS TOBACCO AND POTATO AT COURT OF ELIZABETH I

- The Sun: Queen Says "Great Shag, Walter"
- **The Monte Carlo Times: Rothmans to sponsor Raleigh**
- The Sunday Sport: Alien Spud Stole My Fags
- **The Lancet: Cigarettes Cure All Known Diseases**
- OK! magazine: Queen's Potato Goes Out
- **The Guardian: Raleigh Helps Queen To Cross Poodle**
- The London Evening Standard: Tuber Strike Off
- **The Financial Times: Chancellor Admits May Have Blundered With Tax On Potatoes Scheme**

GOD CREATES UNIVERSE

- The Telegraph: Universe Manufacturer Goes Out Of Business After Six Days
- **The Times: Nothing Happened Yesterday**
- The Daily Star: "I'm Over The Moon" Says God
- **The Daily Star: Would You Adam & Eve It!**
- The Lancet: BMA Warn Rib Transplants Can Cause Lumps On Chest
- **The Irish Times: Genesis Good For You**
- The Daily Mail: Spot The Apple And Win A Skoda
- **The Daily Mail: Snake Problem At Theme Park – Last Two Visitors Forced To Leave**
- Bookbinder's Weekly: Adam Invents Loose Leaf System

Costcutters

The BBC has for many years been famed for its extravagance with licence payers' money. Humph himself became so incensed by it that he personally instructed the BBC to stop putting chilled champagne in his dressing room. He said there was simply no point in going to the expense of chilling it if it was only going in the bath. The teams' response has been to suggest some low-budget versions of popular films, books, radio and television programmes ...

- Sink The Bookmark
- **Pushing Miss Daisy**
- Still There With The Wind
- **Oklahomeless**
- The Polaroid Of Dorian Grey
- **Gulliver's Cheap Day Return**
- Down And Out In Beverley Nichols
- **Mozart's Così fan one-te**
- Le Miserable
- **Twin Peak**
- Gibbon's Decline And Fall Of The Hackney Empire
- **E M Forster's A Passage To Islington**
- A A Milne's classic Winnie the Number Ones
- **John Buchan's The Step**
- *Animal Hospital* to become Animal Six-month Waiting List
- **Neighbour, Eastender, Coronation Bedsit and Emmerdale Allotment**
- Chekhov's The Sister and The Cherry Bowl
- *The Deerhunter* **becomes The Mousetrap**
- Jerome K Jerome's One Man In A Rubber Ring
- **Bleak Shed**
- Dogend, Prince Of Denmark
- **Catcher In The Muesli**
- The Dicken's classic – Dombey
- **Sex, Lies And Pop-Up Books**
- Set in Oxford – Inspector Less
- **The Camomile Tea Bag**
- Cecil B de Mille's *Ten Commandments* to be re-done as Cecil B de Snack's Three And A Half Suggestions
- **Annie Get Your Stick**
- Charlie And The Chocolate Biscuit
- **Joseph And His Amazing Beige Cardigan**
- Kevin Costner's Dances With Aston Villa
- **Around The Block In Eighty Days**
- *The Big Sleep* is now The Little Knap
- **Tinker, Tailor, Soldier, Peeping Tom**

- The National Pottery
- **The musical *Buddy* to be re-done as Casual Acquaintance and *Miss Saigon* as Avoid Dagenham**
- A Streetcar Named Vaguely Interested
- **Only Horses**
- A Dance To The Music Of Tim
- **Thomas The Tank Top**
- Jane Austen's Pride & Precious Little Else
- **Hancock's Five Minutes**
- Absolutely Nebulous
- **The Pocket Money Programme**
- To The Semi Born
- **Clive Anderson Talks Less**
- Watchpuppy
- **Mission Perfectly Feasible**
- The Great Grimsby
- **The Lunchpack Of Notre Dame**
- Ready Steady Pot Noodle
- **The Water Pistols Of Navarone**
- Gunfight At The Less Than Satisfactory Coral
- **Conan The Librarian**
- Those Magnificent Men With Their Sewing Machines
- **Samson And The Lilo**
- The Madness Of Thora Hird
- **A Tale Of Two Citrus Fruits ("It was the best of limes it was the worst of limes")**
- Nanouk Of The North Circular

- **One Dalmatian**
- Conan Doyle's The Adventures Eamon Holmes
- **A Room With A Loo**
- The Great Escalope
- **The Magnificent 7-Up**
- The Old Curiosity Car Boot Sale
- *Starlight Express* **becomes Network Southeast**
- Lady Chatterley's Pen Pal
- **Challenge Anna Karenina**
- A remake of *Marathon Man* called Snickers Man
- **And *Mastermind* with Peter Snow**

Humphs Pick of Parlour Games

Here are two excellent parlour games that I vividly remember playing back in those bygone days when you could leave the door open at all hours and the whole family would huddle round a roaring fire. I still don't understand why we didn't just shut the door ...

HUNT THE SLIPPER

A diverting old Victorian parlour game which caused much excitement when I first suggested it to the *I'm Sorry I Haven't A Clue* teams as they thought I'd said "Hump The Stripper". The man who was in to take the paint off the door frames got quite agitated as well. In "Hunt The Slipper", the chairman sits with his eyes closed while the slipper is passed around behind the players' backs. After a few seconds' slipper passing, he'll call out: "Slipper search on!" and then open his eyes. Obviously he'll have no idea where the slipper is, but the players should keep passing the slipper around secretly and he'll have to guess who is holding the slipper, and challenge them by pointing and calling out: "Slipper holder!". If he guesses correctly, the slipper holder must declare: "Yes, slipper holder I".

(For added entertainment value, it is recommended that this game is played without a slipper.)

WINKING

Another favourite pastime of mine was "Winking" – at least I think that's what it was called. These are the rules. There are four chairs arranged in a semi-circle. A player sits on each chair, except for one, which is kept empty. Behind each chair, including the empty one, one player should stand with his hands resting on the chair, but not touching the player sitting on it. The player standing behind the empty chair starts the game by winking at one of his sitting team-mates. The team-mate who is winked at must try to leave his chair and dash to an empty one. The player standing behind him however, must try to stop him from going by putting his hands on his shoulders, and if he does this quickly enough, the player in the chair must remain where he is until he is winked at again. If he manages to get away, the player who failed to keep him must wink at someone else to fill his chair. After the sitters have been winked at, the sitters stand and wink at the standers, who are now sitting.

(It's best to play this game while the rules are being read out as there is usually insufficient time to do both in the one evening.)

Unclaimed Prizes

All of these fabulous prizes have been available to the winners of our regular "Pick Up Song" competition. They are amazingly high quality, amazingly valuable financially and, amazingly, totally unwanted ...

- Something to suit the homeowner who doesn't like to be kept awake by the furniture – a lovely de-caffeinated coffee table.

- **Just the thing for the aspiring athlete to keep an unruly carpet in check – a set of anabolic stair-rods.**

- From the new Findus dermatolgy convenience range – a boil in the bag.

- **Something so comfortable to sit on it'll make you feel like royalty – a Parker-Bowles recliner.**

- A boon for the dog-loving handyman – a set of adjustable spaniels.

- **For the alfresco-eating pet lover – a lovely picnic hamster.**

- Allowing the most inveterate of sleep-walkers to wander unencumbered – some state-of-the-art cordless pyjamas.

- **From the Duchess of York's hair care range – a year's supply of Wash 'n' Go Ski-ing.**

- To enable you to enjoy a never-ending supply of eggs for an environmentally sound breakfast – a rechargeable battery hen.

- **An ideal choice for the food lover who can never remember what he likes for pudding – a tin of Amnesia Creamed Rice.**

- The latest addition to our new range of transcendental furniture – an occasional table.

- **Ideal for the Jamaican DIY enthusiast – a Desmond Dekker workmate.**

- An expenses-paid trip to see England play the first Test at Lourdes. And if they're not all out by lunch, also witness a miracle.

BARRY CRYER

Yorkshireman Barry originally came to London from Leeds. where he appeared at the Windmill theatre in London. but was turned away at the door for being under-age. He then went on to write for almost every top comic until. one by one. they drifted off to night class to learn to write for themselves. He is now the country's leading Comedy Antiquarian and over the years many top-flight comedians in search of material have flocked to Barry's kiosk outside Waterloo Station. His many fans (along with his collection of chopsticks and kimonos) are on loan to the V&A.

"When people who write about radio and people who listen to radio are in agreement about a programme. it must be doing something right. So the return of the show that won the gong for best radio programme from both the *Broadcasting Press Guild* and the *Voice of the Viewer and Listener* is a rare occasion for unmitigated joy."
Peter Barnard, *The Times*

"The constant sound of the radio was my greatest comfort... There was a comedy quiz with Willie Rushton. Tim Brooke-Taylor. Barry Cryer and Graeme Garden which made me laugh out loud. I thought to myself: "Look at you. the situation you're in and you're laughing!""
Stephanie Slater (kidnap victim imprisoned in coffin) *The Sun*

GRAEME GARDEN

Doctor Graeme's Aberdonian roots are dyed a pleasing flesh colour. In 1968. while waiting in a queue for treatment at King's College Hospital. he carelessly qualified as a doctor. His first diagnosis – "This is certainly not the job for me" – probably saved more lives than even his kindest tutor ever envisaged. Since then he has written a great deal. and some of it still hasn't washed off. A late television flowering on *If I Ruled the World* has brought him to the attention of a whole new generation of blissfully ignorant viewers. The original idea for *I'm Sorry I Haven't a Clue* was Graeme's. but he generously refuses to take all the blame.

"The show captures the spirit of the times for those people who think that modern life
– or at least those parts of it reflected in the media – is all show and no substance"
Roland White, *The Radio Times*

HUMPHREY LYTTELTON

Grey-haired. bespectacled. trumpet-playing Humphrey was born in Eton. near Slough. He is believed to be the first grey-haired. bespectacled. trumpet-playing baby to be born there. He served in the Guards and, on VE Day. he played outside Buckingham Palace until his arrest. He became Chairman of *I'm Sorry I Haven't A Clue* thanks to his close friendship with the then Prime Minister. Clement Attlee. Humph has no letters after his name. but several behind the sideboard. His hobbies are calligraphy and collecting photographs of Fourth Division football clubs' corner flags. He is a legend.

" 'Finsbury Park' said backwards comes out as 'Crappy Rubsniff'. Any radio programme which alerts you to this one-in-a-million serendipity must be worth the licence fee ..."
Julie Myerson, *The Observer*

"There is a certain feeling of communal merriment and gladness-to-be-British which only comes when one is tuned into *I'm Sorry I Haven't A Clue*"
Ysenda Maxtone-Graham, *Sunday Telegraph*

"It's very like watching a good jazz band play – the pleasure lies in hearing the improvisations grow from nothing ... It's the sound of time wasting."
Stephen Pile, *Daily Telegraph*

TIM BROOKE-TAYLOR

Tim hails from Buxton in Derbyshire. In the 1960s he went to Cambridge. and had a very enjoyable day. While there. he read Law and Economics. and some even longer words as well. He later went for a job with Dolcis as he had a great interest in Shoe Business. Unfortunately. due to a spelling mistake in his application form. he ended up in Show Business. Tim has appeared on many radio programmes. and has also been heard on television. Notably he was in *The Goodies* and in *You Must Be The Star's Husband* – in which he took the title role! Tim is currently staring at the Theatre Royal. Drury Lane.